LOCAL TRAVEL GUIDE TO MOLDOVA

OLGA STAN

OPPIAN

Published by Oppian Press
Helsinki, Finland

ISBN 978-951-877-181-7

1. INTRODUCTION.

Before visiting Moldova have a look at the information inside. It will help you get a glimpse of what you are going to experience by visiting this small, unknown but amazing country. Moldova is the country which has been least impacted by the tourism that is why strangers are still welcomed with hospitality and friendships are easy to form. Moldova is a secret garden, authentic in every detail and this guide aims to help you discover and enjoy the most of it.

Let's see what's to discover!

2. History:

The Moldovan feudal state was formed in 1359; Bogdan 1st is considered to be its founder. After the formation of the feudal state, the most prosperous political and economic development period was the 15th century, particularly between 1457 and 1504, the years of reign of Stefan the Great

Towards the middle of the 15th century, the suzerainty regime was established by the Otoman Empire. In 1775, the Ottoman Empire concedes the North-Western part of Moldova (later named Bucovina), to the Habsburg Empire. In 1812, as a result of the Russian-Turkish war (1806-1812), the Eastern part of Moldova, situated between the Prut and the Dniester rivers, was annexed by the Russian Empire and a new province named Bessarabia was formed. In 1859 the Principality of Moldova united with Wallachia in one state, later named Romania.

After the revolution of February 1917, the hostilities between Russia and the central powers of Bessarabia began. From the 23 to 27 of October 1917, the city council of Chisinau proclaimed the autonomy of Bessarabia and the formation of Sfatul Tarii (Parliamen of Bessarabia province) as a legislative body. On 27 March 1918 Sfatul Tarii, as a legislative body of the Moldovan Democratic Republic, voted for the union with Romania in 1918.

In June 1940, in the context of the pact between Hitler and Stalin the Soviet Union issued an ultimatum to Romania concerning the annexation of Bessarabia, Northern Bucovina and Herta region of Moldova between Carpathians and Prut. Two thirds of Bessarabia were joined with Transnistria in order to establish the Soviet Socialist Republic of Moldova.

The Republic of Moldova declared its independence on 27 August 1991. On 2 March 1992, the Republic of Moldova adhered to the United Nations Organization, and on 29 July 1994 it adopted the Constitution.

Among the main events that took place after the independence were the joining of the United Nations Organization and the approval of the Constitution, in the modern history of Republic of Moldova, the liberalization of the visa regime with the European Union member states on 28 April 2014, and the signing of the Association Agreement with the European Union on 27 June 2014.

3. Geographical Position:

Moldova is a small but unique and charming country, tucked away between Romania and Ukraine in the furthest reaches of Eastern Europe. On the map it looks like bunch of ripe grapes which is no coincidence: Moldova has the highest percentage in the world of lands dedicated to vineyards. Looking for more than just magnets to take home with you from your trips? You've chosen the right destination. As one of the least visited countries in the world, Moldova will surprise and intrigue you at every turn, leaving you with unforgettable memories and unique stories to tell your friends. Moldova is situated in the south-eastern part of European continent. Most of its territory lies between the area's two main rivers, Dniester and Prut and covers an area of 33,843 km^2, ranking 32nd in Europe. The Dniester forms a small part of Moldova's border with Ukraine in the northeast and southeast, but it mainly flows through the eastern part of the country, separating Bessarabia and Transnistria. The Prut River forms Moldova's entire western boundary with Romania. The Danube touches the Moldovan border at its southernmost tip, and forms the border for 200 m (656 ft). Moldova extends over 350 km from the north to the south, and 150 km from the west to the east. Extreme points of Moldova are:

Northernmost point – village Naslavcea (48*29 N latitude)

Southernmost point – village Giurgiulesti (45*28* N latitude)

Westernmost point – Criva village (26*30*E longitude)

Easternmost point – the village Palanca (30*05* E longitude)

4. Population:

The estimated population is 4,35 million inhabitants, the average population density is 129 inhabitants per square km. When speaking about ethnic groups, about three-fourths of Moldova's population consists of ethnic Moldovans. There are smaller populations, like: Ukrainians, Russians, Gagauz, Roma (Gypsies), and Bulgarians. The Ukrainian population of Moldova, the largest minority group, is divided between those who are native to the country (their ancestors having farmed for centuries in what is now Moldova) and those who migrated to Moldova during the periods of Russian and Soviet control. The former group makes up the majority of Ukrainians in Moldova. Moldova's Russian population arrived during the periods of Russian imperial and Soviet rule, usually as civil servants and labourers. The Gagauz, mainly rural people, have lived on the Bugeac Plain since the late 18th century. The country's ethnic Bulgarians also are mainly rural and inhabit the southern districts, where they settled at the end of the 18th century. Only a small percentage of Moldovan citizens identify themselves as Roma.

5. Religion:

During the period of Soviet rule, the influence of churches in Moldovan public life was limited by the religious policy imposed by the Communist Party of the Soviet Union separation of church and state, exclusion of the churches from education, and subjection of the faithful to atheistic propaganda. Since the collapse of the Soviet Union, however, all churches have undergone a revival and have striven to regain their former prominence. The overwhelming majority of ethnic Moldovans, Russians, Gagauz, and Ukrainians are Eastern Orthodox Christians. There are also other Christians and smaller Muslim and Jewish communities. The Jewish community is overwhelmingly urban and began to enter present-day Moldova in substantial numbers after 1800, but its numbers have been greatly reduced by wars, pogroms, the Holocaust, and emigration (since the creation of the Moldovan republic, there has been considerable emigration of Jews to Russia, Ukraine, and Israel). Less than one-tenth of Moldova's residents consider themselves nonreligious.

6. Language:

The official language in Moldova is Romanian, which is the native language of 80.2% of the population. Although there is a language ping pong in Moldova. The Declaration of Independence of the Republic of Moldova (1991) named Romanian the official language of the new formed state – the Republic of Moldova. In 1994, the Constitution of the Republic of Moldova claimed that the national language of Moldova is Moldovan, based on the Latin alphabet. In 2013, the Constitutional Court of Moldova decided that the Declaration of Independence takes precedence over the Constitution and the state language is Romanian. However, the Moldovan Parliament members have not yet amended the text of Art.13 of the Constitution. The phrase "Romanian language" will be introduced in the Constitution if at least 67 Parliament members support the draft law.

Russian (language of interethnic communication), Gagauz (a Turkish dialect) spoken by the Gagauz people of Moldova and it is the official language of the Autonomous Region of Gagauzia in Moldova.

7. The mineral resources:

The mineral resources of the Republic of Moldova are mainly represented by sedimentary rocks, such as limestone, chalk, gypsum, sand, sandstone, bentonite, tripoli, and diatomite, which can be used in construction, cement and glass production, food processing, chemical and metallurgical industries etc. Among other nonmetallic minerals that have been identified on the territory of the Republic of Moldova are graphite, phosphorite, zeolite, fluorite, barite, iodine and bromine as well as several industrial metals such as iron, lead, zinc and copper. Moldova has small deposits of lignite, crude oil and natural gas. The soil cover of Moldova is fertile and various consisting of more than 745 varieties. Chernozem (Russian: black earth) occupies around three-fourth of the land area of the country. Brown and gray forest soils cover around 11% of the country's land area. Floodplain, or alluvial, meadow soils occupy around 12% of the land area of Moldova.

8. Climate:

The climate of the Republic of Moldova is moderately continental. It is characterized by a lengthy frost-free period, short mild winters, lengthy hot summers, modest precipitation, and long dry periods in the south. The average annual temperature increases southward from around 8-9°C in the north to around 10-11°C in the south. When it is the best time to visit Moldova? Well it is always a good time, as you can see there are all four seasons and no matter if you plan a vacation in winter, Spring, Summer or Autumn there are lots of activities to enjoy, places to visit and people to meet. There is so much for visitors to love in Moldova. The countryside is green and tranquil. The pace of life is peaceful and unhurried. Conviviality and hospitality is what characterizes the Moldovans. Moldovans have a love of tradition and rich history, preserved today in ancient fortresses, exquisitely decorated churches and living monasteries.

9. Countryside:

Moldova is a country that has been protected from industrialization. The uncontaminated air and the ecologic habitat will create a pleasant atmosphere of spiritual relaxation for you. The positive energy gained during your stay will be physically and emotionally invigorating you for a long time. The multitude of natural reserves, the relief with hills and plains, with rivers and lakes, with cliffs and knolls, covered with secular forests and wine plantations will carry you to a sensational world.

10. Culture, Folk Music, Dance and Art:

Moldova has been settled by many people throughout history, resulting in a rich mix of cultural, religious, architectural, and culinary traditions. Moldovan traditional culture is widely celebrated in music, dance and art. Classical music, jazz and fine art compliment traditional attractions can be enjoyed at events, concerts or celebrations throughout the year.

Moldovans widely celebrate traditional music and dance. There are literally hundreds of songs which follow the tempo of traditional dances such as the Hora and Sirba. The melodies are light and playful and are played to a toe tapping rhythm. The dances are typically performed in a circle with the dancers holding hands or linking arms while dancer in a counter clockwise direction.

From ancient times, on the territory of Moldova there have been practiced diverse types of popular arts, such as: pottery, egg incrustation, carpet weaving, wood and stone processing, artistic metal processing. The aspiration towards beauty and harmony were reflected from ancient times not only by embellishing the interiors of the houses but also the tradition of adorning the clothes, the popular costume. This custom of adorning clothes, table clothes and ritual tissues (towels) called Prosop is practiced in each rural locality and persists until nowadays. Once a year and usually in summer you can visit the Festival Ia Mania which is organised in Holercani. And there you can see the most beautiful adorned clothes but also different kind of handmade art. If you'd like to get more info and pictures about this festival you just have to Google: Ia Mania.

Carpets are considered works of art in Moldova; they represent an expression of national creativity and identity. In communication we use the work carpet to sum up all the thick fabrics. Their colours are naturally obtained from plants. The motifs are floral and vegetal. According to the tradition the carpets were used as a part of the bride's dowry and were put in the house to emit energy and well-being in the family. Passed along from generation to generation, the carpet weaving technique from Romania and Moldova is a part of the UNESCO Intangible Cultural Heritage starting with December 1, 2016.

11. Cuisine:

It's the people that make Moldova special! Travel to any corner of Moldova and you will find genuine, friendly interactions with warm and open people. When you arrive in a Moldovan village, before you know it you will be at a table groaning with food, and with the host treating you to local wine. Our national cuisine will surprise you with its honesty, simplicity and richness. Close your eyes and dream of a savoury soup called Zeamă, cooked with homemade noodles, and

Mămăliga - a dish made from cornmeal - which is cut with a thread and served with Moldovan cheese, sour cream and a meat stew, Tocană. Our special pies, Plăcintele, are prepared from a thin, flaky pastry with a variety of fillings: cabbage, cottage cheese, apple, pumpkin or cherry – the choice is yours! Is your mouth watering yet? If you're not overwhelmed by the warmth of our people, then it's our food that will win your heart.

Moldovan cuisine offers an incredible variety. Culinary influences include: Turkish, Russian, Ukranian, Greek, Jewish and German. Traditional holiday dishes include cabbage leaves stuffed with minced meat called Sarmale, meat jelly called "Racituri" and noodles with chicken. The holiday table is usually decorated with baked items, such as pastries, cakes, rolls, buns with a variety of fillings (cheese, fruit, vegetables, walnuts etc).

Traditional for the autochthon cuisine is the food prepared from the most diverse vegetables, grown in ecological conditions on the fertile lands of chernozem (black earth) of the rural households. The vegetables are baked, stewed, pickled or marinated, thus becoming real culinary works of art.

12. Time:

The Republic of Moldova is situated in the Eastern European time zone, 2 hours ahead of Greenwich Mean Time (GMT +2, summer time GMT +3.)

13. Currency:

The national currency of the Republic of Moldova is Moldovan Leu (MDL). The credit cards are accepted in banks, hotels, travel agencies and shops. The banks are open from 09:00 am to 16:00pm from Monday to Friday. You can exchange money in any bank; usually they have the highest rate and don't take any commission. Also you can exchange at exchange offices just pay attention at the rates and commissions. Some exchange offices may take 2% commission.

14. Visa:

Citizens of EU Member States, the Principality of Monaco, the Republic of San Marino, the Swiss Confederation and the Holy See do not need a visa to enter the territory of Moldova for a stay of up to 90 days.

15. Useful Information:

Electricity: 220V(230), 50Hz, standard electrical Sockets with two pins of European continental type.

Telephone country code: +373, code of Chisinau municipality (22), internet domain: md.

112 – The unique number for urgencies: Police, medical urgencies, ambulance and fire services.

Briceni
Lipcani
Edinet
Soroca
Drocjia
Transnistria
Costesti
Balti
Ribnita
MOLDOVA
UKRAINE
Falesti
Cornesti
Orhei
Dubasari
Ungheni
Straseni
Transnistria
CHISINAU
Ialoveni
Singera
Bender
Hincesti
Tiraspol
Causeni
Cimislia
Olanesti
Leova
ROMANIA
Comrat
Ceadir
Lunga
UKRAINE
Cahul
Taraclia
Vulcanesti

THE CAPITAL

1. CHISINAU

When you will plan your trip to Moldova, most probably you will decide to stay in Chisinau, which is the capital of Republic of Moldova.

Chisinau is located on seven hills in the neighbourhood of the river Bîc, being one of the oldest and the most important localities in Moldova.

First mentions of this city appeared in 1466. For a long time Chisinau has been a boyar patrimony. Today this is a large historical and cultural center. You can see ancient buildings built in medieval times, although you don't have an "old town" as almost all capitals do. Each year new modern buildings appear here.

Organ Hall and National Drama Theatre located opposite to it are the main cultural sights of the city. Between these sights is located Great National Gathering Square – the biggest and most beautiful square in Chisinau. Victory Square is located in the center of the city. This square is built in the honour of a famous commander Kutuzov who has defeated Turkish troops. A park is located near the square, Stefan cel Mare Central Park. If you make a walk in the park, you will reach one of the most important religious sights of the city – the Cathedral. This church was built in 1830.

Church of the Nativity of the Virgin is a great example of old-style architecture. One of the halls of this church has been turned into an exhibition center. Pushkin House-Museum is also a place worth visiting while in Chisinau. This building is quite usual at a glance, but the museum exhibits an interesting collection of items that will tell you about the life and work of the great poet. So called Valley of Classics situated in the Stefan cel Mare Central Park will get you acquainted with great Moldavian writers. The valley honours famous poets and novelists of the country by featuring their statues made of granite. Theatre connoisseurs will never get bored in Chisinau as in this city you will find a large number of cultural facilities – Opera and Ballet Theatre, Theatre for Children named Luceafarul, Doll's Theatre Licurici and much more.

A landmark for Chisinau's historical site is the Holy Gate, also known under another name - the Arch of Victory. This arch is located in the heart of the city, which was built in 1840. It has a massive bell, the weight of which is more than 6 tons. This huge bell was cast from melted Turkish cannons. This historical monument looks very impressive.

The oldest building in Chisinau is Mazarache Church, which was built in the middle of the 13th century. The history of this church is inextricably linked with the name of the city treasurer Vasile Mazarachi, on whose personal means it was built. Despite the fact that the history of the existence of this church had to go through many reconstructions, it managed to retain its original appearance almost completely. In the walls of the church there are also many interesting artefacts.

2. Parks:

The city has a lot of beautiful places for walking. One of the most picturesque is Stefan cel Mare Central Park. It was founded in 1818 and occupies a vast territory of 7 hectares. This park is remarkable not only for its natural beauties. On its territory there are many beautiful monuments. In the warm season in the park, there are gorgeous fountains. It is loved not only by the guests of the city, but also by the locals. Other great parks to spend time outdoors you can find almost in any part of the city, not only in the center. Go for a evening walk or a morning run in the park Valea Trandafirilor, you will enjoy the silent view of three lakes in the heart of the park and a huge variety of roses of all colours. There are also different activities organised for children in the park. Also take time to visit botanical garden Gradina Botanica, it is a nice park with a lot of species of trees, plants, flowers. You can spend the whole day there maybe even organize a picnic, although no barbeque is allowed there. Another great park for a walk and a picnic is Dendrarium Park. Valea Morilor Park is not as big as the rest but if you walk along you get to the biggest exhibition center in Moldova, MoldExpo. Lots of interesting exhibitions are organised there, while in Moldova search for the

MoldExpo program, maybe you'll get to visit an exhibition of your taste and interest.

3. Museums:

An ordinary walk through the city will allow you to get acquainted with its outstanding architectural sights. On the central avenue, you can see the impressive building of the main post office, which was built in the middle of the 19th century. Once it was decorated with a huge glass globe, which was destroyed during the earthquake in 1976. This element was not restored.

Fans of hiking in interesting museums, should take a look at the National Museum of Archeology and History of Moldova. It also occupies an incredibly beautiful historical building. Now the museum's fund has about 260,000 unique exhibits. A significant part of them was discovered during the excavation directly on the territory of the republic. In the museum, visitors can see samples of ancient weapons, household items, ornaments and decorative objects. In addition to the archeological exhibits themselves, the museum houses a collection of old books, photographs, paintings and historical documents.

National Museum of Ethnography and Natural History - this is the oldest museum in Bessarabia it was founded in the 19th Century on the on the basis of the exhibits of the Agricultural Exhibition in 1889.

National Museum of Fine Arts – here you can enjoy the works of painting, graphics, sculpture, decorative art, numismatics and medal art, by their value and the names of the authors who created them, allow a clear picture of the development of the plastic arts in the country as well as around the world, starting with the ancient period at the end of the twentieth century.

National Museum of History - The exhibition illustrates the history of Moldova from the oldest times to the present, which shows cultural, economic, political, and social development of the human society in this geographic area in different historical times. This is a must see! You won't regret it.

Museum of the City of Chisinau - the museum is located in an old water tower and offers many exhibits concerning the city and the country, plus you'll get the chance to enjoy a great view from the top.

Museum Alexandr Pushkin - It's a lovely museum, with information in Romanian and Russian (and some in English) about Pushkin and his contemporaries, with some cool exhibits (eg drafts of manuscripts, writing desk, house life of the time).

The museum holds many original manuscripts of poems that Pushkin wrote or started while living here: "Bakhchisaraiskii Fontan," "Tsygany," and most notably the beginning sections of the magnificent EUGENE ONEGIN."

Military Museum – It is worth visiting this museum especially if you are interested in the 1992 civil war, communism, the 2nd World War, Stalin and everything else that Moldova has endured.

4. Shopping in Chisinau:

It's best to start shopping in Chisinau from visiting shopping malls, and the largest one in town is Shopping MallDova. The large-scale shopping complex occupies a huge four-story building, within the walls of which are shops of famous brands, as well as restaurants and cafes of different specializations and even a cinema Patria. Here you will find Aridon, Jennifer, Miss Sixty, and United Colors ready to please ladies, as well as Celio and Franttini stores where all men should go. Besides that, the shopping mall houses a number of excellent sports and shoe stores, and one of the largest cosmetics stores in town – INA center.

Jumbo is an equally popular shopping center based in another beautiful four-story building featuring a spectacular facade. About 60 shops of various directions operate in this shopping center, and their convenient thematic division by floors makes walking around the mall really comfortable. On the lower level are furniture and household stores, and the second floor is devoted to children's products. On the third floor are popular clothing and shoe stores, and on the fourth, you can find restaurants, cafes, and all kinds of entertainment facilities.

Elat Shopping Center is perfect for families, as a large part of its stores are aimed at ladies and children. On the first floor are interesting shops focusing on cosmetics, accessories, perfumes and gift products. This shopping center is famous for the variety of clothing and shoe stores offering attractive prices, as well as budget restaurants and cafes.

Soiuz is another mall with its special features; it is very popular with fans of modern branded clothing. Ladies will be able to visit elite underwear shops or buy quality cosmetics from well-known manufacturers. For visitors with children, here there are several shops full of children's clothes and toys. This shopping center is mainly aimed at wealthy customers, offering them a great solarium and a beauty salon.

Most popular brand stores are concentrated in Sun City Shopping Center. It is located in a lively central area of Chisinau, near popular shopping streets and entertainment facilities. The mall houses a number of elite cosmetics shops, excellent designer boutiques where you can pick exclusive clothes and accessories.

For those who aren't ready to spend a lot on new outfits and cosmetics, the best option is to visit Gemenii. This is quite a small shopping center occupying a beautiful historic building. Shops operating here are notable for reasonable prices. On the first floor, ladies will appreciate a large store with decorative and caring cosmetics. One the same floor, one can find many men's and women's fashion shops.

UNIC is a four-floor commercial center situated on the main boulevard Stefan cel Mare. Here is the only place where you can shop clothes made in Moldova. Moldova has a lot of young talented designers. Local brands have created a community named Din Inima which means from the heart. Here you can see and even buy Moldovan national clothes "Ie" this is a shirt embroidered with floral and vegetal motifs.

Atrium and Grand Hall are two small shopping centers where you can enjoy shopping for presents, jewelery, cosmetics, perfumes but also women and men clothes. In Atrium you can have a drink on the terrace which is located on the roof of the shopping center, the feeling and the view is amazing.

Chisinau has several large markets, among which the Central Market is considered the most vibrant one. Locals and tourists go here in search of cheap clothing, household goods, as well as popular local foods. At the Central Market, you can find several stalls with souvenirs, which can be bought here much cheaper than in many shopping malls.

Not far from the city center there is the so-called Artists Alley where the city's best artists and craftsmen present their works in the open air.

Here you can choose ready-made magnificent paintings or order your own portrait. In addition to paintings, in the alley, they sell interesting jewelry and bijouterie, as well as popular handmade souvenirs.

These are the big shopping centers but when walking on the main boulevard, Stefan cel Mare – you will see a huge number of small shops which offer a huge variety of products for all the tastes and pockets.

Another interesting place to shop is the Yard Sale. Yard sale is one of a kind on Moldova as it is an event that happens every 2 months offering a combination of shopping handmade things by locals and artists, clothing, a variety of food, music and workshops for kids and adults. During the warmer seasons their events happen outside in nature, while colder months inside various buildings. Every event they change their location and their theme which allows you to experience different parts of the city, as well discover different foods and styles. Yard Sale gives a glimpse into the local food, culture, tastes and trends.

Besides open marked and yard sale of course you can stick to what you are used what concerns shopping for food. In Chisinau you will find a chain of supermarkets with a great variety of food and hygiene products at decent prices. They are located all over the city: Furchette, GreenHill, Hypermaket N1, Linela Market also you will find small food shops opened even till later than the big supermarkets.

5. Places to eat – best restaurants:

Chisinau has a rich variety of dining destinations in the city; there are places from a luxurious gourmet restaurant to a modest family cafe. Within the historic district of the city there is an international restaurant **Pegas** that has repeatedly won honorary awards for the quality of dishes. Spacious room of the restaurant is decorated in a classical style. The restaurant often hosts performances of famous bands in the evening. The main feature of the restaurant is delicious French cuisine prepared by chef's own recipes.

Fans of European cuisine would be interested in visiting **Beer House** restaurant, which always attracts a large number of beer lovers. In addition to the excellent beer, there is a wide selection of German and French dishes on the menu and several national dishes too. In the warmer months, the restaurant moves a portion of tables on the beautiful terrace. Beer House serves visitors until late in the evening.

Popasul Dacilor - This rustic restaurant is set in an old manner house, and is one of Chișinău's true gastronomic culinary delights. Popasul Dacilor is a gateway to the traditional Moldavian roots not only in culinary diversity but also in its authentic and unique decor. Popasul Dacilor takes its guests for a virtual journey back in time, with delicious dishes harking back to a by-gone era. Waitresses are dressed in old-fashioned costume while serving acclaimed local dishes that bring together diverse tastes. Though Popasul Dacilor is praised for its service and constant high quality food, the house's main specialty is not to be missed. The indoor restaurant can seat up to 150 people, while two additional terraces expand its capacity, which, along with the picturesque set make it a perfect choice for all occasions.

Vatra Neamului - has earned its name thanks to providing the best service in town. Owner and designer Mr. Nicolae Avram envisioned a venue where appetite for flavor and culture are both equally satisfied. Vatra Neamului offers Romanian-inspired fish, meat and soup dishes, accompanied by a large wine list. The wooden decor not only gives a luxurious atmosphere to the place, but also gives pride of place to Vatra Neamului's portraits of some of Moldova's greatest poets, writers and artists. This top-notch, truly authentic restaurant offers a number of quiet rooms for a more intimate dining or its terrace for a more flamboyant experience.

Designed to be a homey and cozy venue, Gok-Oguz is the city's only restaurant that specializes in dishes from the southern Gagauz region, as well as a Bulgarian fare. Set in a charming courtyard, the aim of this venue is to make each guest feel at home. You'll find private and semi-private indoor and outdoor seating and exceptional hospitality. Gok-Oguz is known for its lamb specialties.

La Taifas - this acclaimed national restaurant is set in a Moldovan style peasant's house, ensuring that you'll get a real taste of Moldova here. Authentic scenery, Moldavian hospitality, accompanied with traditional dishes, all delivered in accordance with national customs, this is what La Taifas stands for. The restaurant offers a wide choice of specialties, so there's something for everyone. La Taifas is a three-storey building, where the first floor serves as the main eatery, the second as a banquet hall, while the third floor was designed and structured for a romantic, more intimate dining experience. If you're in the mood for *chiorba, mamaliga, placinta* or for excellent local Moldovan wines embraced by national live music, then La Taifas is the perfect venue.

Caravan – is a real cultural gem in Chişinău, is the city's chief Asian restaurant. Caravan is warm and welcoming, ideal for romantic dining. The interior displays organza curtains, rugs, carpets and handmade tableware. The attractive menu lines up a wide choice of veal, lamb, duck, chicken, fish and vegetarian specialties that are complemented by traditional Uzbek brew tea.

View Café & Restaurant - A luxurious venue located on the 8th floor of the Nobil Luxury Boutique Hotel Moldova, View Cafe & Restaurant is Chişinău's only panoramic restaurant that offers a truly scenic view of the city landscape. Besides the fantastic views and elegantly designed terrace seating, View Café & Restaurant makes sure the food delivers an upscale dining experience as well. Their kitchen emphasizes a fusion of French and Italian tastes, yet with a local twist;

therefore, the menu lines up a great range of eclectic choices that change seasonally. Gentle, live piano music and impeccable service amplify the pleasant atmosphere further.

Tucano Cofee - this is Chişinău's best-loved hub for light meals, boasting its own high-quality 100% Arabica coffee brand. With its mission statement 'Love, Peace and Coffee,' Tucano Coffee aims to offer a platform where cultures can freely mingle together under one roof and differences are accepted and respected; this is augmented by their attentive personnel and the cosmopolitan, hippie-styled design. Guests can choose from a rich variety of coffee specialties, accompanied by delicious sweets and savories as well as light breakfast and lunch options. If you're looking for the best cheesecakes in town then don't miss Tucano, which offers several different flavors. The venue is also home to regular cultural events, from photo exhibitions to pantomimes shows, and painting events led by local artists.

Crème de la Crème - This three storey culinary heaven boasts the city's best desserts choices, however Creme de la Crème is also an ideal lunch and dinner venue. The restaurant owners set the scene for the patisserie in a authentic Parisian-style hall located on the ground floor, while the main restaurant gives its guests to a traditional Provençal feel. Besides Creme de la Crème's lauded French croissants and Viennese coffees, the restaurant also offers great variants of salad, pasta and steak plates, leaving guests with an eclectic European menu at an affordable price. Creme de la Crème is an ideal place for weekend brunches and official dining for families and business people alike.

Morimoto Sushi - is a name to remember. Praised for its signature dishes, the restaurant presents an outstanding selection of Japanese and Thai plates at affordable prices. Besides the typical sushi and noodle specialties, Morimoto offers seafood, steak and grill tastes as well. The restaurant's top-level quality both for its service and dishes have justly elevated it to sit among the best international cuisine venues in

Chișinău. Their concept of serving only the freshest and healthiest tastes is warmly welcomed by guests, who can enjoy pleasant indoors or al fresco terrace dining.

El Paso - is a Mexican venue where tastes are rich and aromas are abundant. All ingredients are directly imported from Mexico to ensure complete authenticity, offering the best quesadilla and fajitas in the city. El Paso is a great venue for guests who are fond of hot and spicy dishes that can be washed down by an excellent Mexican Corona beer. Inside the decor is exuberantly Latin and original Mexican articles decorate the walls. As the warmer months arrive, El Paso opens its terrace for an enchanting al fresco dining experience.

Panna Cotta - Centrally located close to the must-see Cathedral Park, Panna Cotta is an excellent choice for those in the mood to sample the familiar and irresistible tastes of Italian cuisine. Very popular among locals for its dessert specialities and dishes prepared with fresh organic ingredients, Panna Cotta also has stylish contemporary interiors that offer a much-deserved break from the hustle of the city. The menu includes a consistent selection of desserts, but also refreshing breakfasts, salads, soups and the traditional polenta with cheese as one of the most attractive main courses.

Vinoteca Wine Room & Restaurant - A recent addition to Chișinău's list of top culinary venues, Vinoteca Wine Room & Restaurant is a must for wine enthusiasts. With impressive decor, this gourmet restaurant is the place to go for guests wishing to experience upscale service and a rich menu with contemporary European dishes, accompanied by the very best local and international wines. Centrally located – just steps away from the Cathedral Park – Vinoteca Wine Room & Restaurant is no doubt one of the city's unmissable culinary attractions.

Chianti - Situated in the heart of the city, Chianti is far more than a simple brunch place. Comprising a restaurant, a bar and a wine shop, Chianti is a great place to try all day. Visit it to relax and enjoy high quality in the most elegant spot around.

Loft - Divided into several areas including a living room, a large hall for non-smokers and a VIP room away from the crowds, Loft is a French bistro with a local touch. The French flair is apparent not only in the interior, but also in the exciting menu that gives you the opportunity to taste some adventurous snacks right in the center of the city.

513 - Although it may prove to be a bit tricky to find, this restaurant is certainly worth the search. It is one of the most fascinating spots in the city and popular among locals and visitors alike, 513 is ideal for a casual brunch with friends providing a great selection of food and drinks. Don't forget to return in the evening to join one of their legendary parties.

La Dolce Italia - is known as the best gelateria in the city, and a visit will explain why. La Doce Italia is proud to offer unique flavors of ice-cream and desserts, originating from the perfect union of Italian culinary traditions and Moldovan fresh products. Taste a crunchy, refreshing cone and if ice-cream is not what you're craving for, order one of their tasty Italian cakes instead.

Caramel - Thanks to some rustic French-style decoration, friendly welcoming smiles and a wide variety of treats, Caramel's sweet world invites you in a fairy tale atmosphere. Whether you prefer a pastry or a light snack, it will definitely exceed your expectations.

Casa Dolce - gives you the chance to taste a Turkish delight in the heart of the city. Do not miss their top-notch baklava and delicious coffee.

La Placinte – It is a place to go with your friends, family and even alone if you want to have a good lunch or dinner. You will be surprised by the pleasant atmosphere good service and delicious traditional food, local wine and beer. The main dishes that you will see in the menu is "Placinte" and that is a must try especially with cheese. A traditional round or square-shaped thin pastry usually filled with soft cheese or apples, cabbage, potatoes and mushrooms etc. is one of the reasons to fall in love with this country. Stop by La Placinte for the most authentic and delicious culinary delights of Moldovan cuisine. The amazing variety of delicious pies will make you want to return to try more. You will find "La Placinte" in each sector of Chisinau, just remember the name.

Andy's Pizza – is a place with quite affordable prices and nice atmosphere. Whether you're feeding a family or fending for yourself, Andy's Pizza will prepare you a perfect meal. Dine-in, eat out, or have it delivered.

Andy's pizza is on Moldavian market for more than 15 years. The service is very good. In the menu, you can find a lot of different dishes for all kind of people. The design is always changing and it is all the time of good quality. The main dish in the menu of course is pizza, you'll find pizza for all tastes, they make even special menu and pizza for kids.

There are a lot of great places to eat and have rest in town you just need to Google and you'll get their location and opening hours.

6. Ideas for Active Rest:

A large selection of entertainment venues, shops and restaurants will enliven your rest and make it even more enjoyable.

If you are a cinema lover then you have to go to one of the following cinemas, that are the best in town: Auto Cinema, Gaudeamus, Odeon,

Patria-Centru Patria Lukoil and Patria MallDova are brightest ones. They are waiting for visitors every day; in addition to bright premieres, favourite old movies are shown there.you can get a ticket to the movie for around 100 lei it depends if it is a premiere or a 3D movie. You can also enjoy 5D movie which is a really great fun especially for kids. Fans of billiards wouldn't find better place to stay than Billard Hall. It is a beautiful club that offers the best atmosphere for recreation. Among other famous billiards clubs Paradis Billiard can be mentioned; it differs with high quality equipment and a cozy atmosphere.

Fans of outdoor recreation have to visit one of the tennis clubs in Chisinau. Both beginners and experienced athletes would find time there enjoyable. Among many local clubs vacationers point out Niagara Club, Tennis Group and Olympia 2000 club. The most famous go-kart center of Chisinau is Formula-Kart; rest here will please both adults and children. Aqua Magic Waterpark – a place for adults and for kids, so if you are travelling with your family this is a great place to escape from the summer heat in the town. Pools available here are suitable for adults and for children of different ages. In the middle of the swimming pool is a good bar. Even those who seem to have tried all possible slides will like water rides presented here. Despite the fact that the water park is quite small, it is very cozy, spacious, and the most important - amusing. On site there is a restaurant where you can dine with the whole family and share impressions from visiting the park.

We should also talk about shops of Chisinau, which are very popular among foreigners. If you are looking for souvenirs, gifts and craft items, the most various choice will be found at the market located opposite the National Theatre, on Stefan cel Mare Street. Ceramics, home textiles, embroidery and antique jewelry are the most popular souvenirs. For those who want to purchase a beautiful picture as a memorable gift, we recommend to go to the Fantezia shop which is not far away from the market. For fresh fruits and vegetables, as well as homemade sweets, it's better to visit the central market; this is where the best home-made cheese pickled vegetables and wine are sold. The wine can also be found in specialty shops. Several attractive shopping pavilions are located in the Elat shopping center.

If sticking to the usual, in Chisinau you will find a chain of supermarkets with a great variety of food, drinks and hygiene products at decent prices. They are located all over the city: Furchette, GreenHill, Hypermaket N1, Linela Market also you will find small food shops opened even till later than the big supermarkets.

Those wishing to increase the extreme hormone to an above-average level can try out such tours as balloon flights. Besides, such a pastime makes the heart tremble not only with the adrenaline rush but also with the magnificent views of Chisinau and its surroundings - the city appears to be so small, like a toy. Equally popular are air tours, during which you can enjoy the same wonderful views sitting in a cockpit. All this will bring an unforgettable experience to travellers who came to Chisinau for some inspiration.

Among entertainment centres, it is worth mentioning Next Level Club appreciated by those looking for a thrill and wishing to solve the task using their wits. Visitors can choose from a few rooms, each of which is decorated on a different theme. Chisinau is also attractive to those who want to learn something new - for example, one can attend drawing classes from Trommigou or Azur-Art. Those wishing to play a team game with their friends (laser tag, paintball) should be advised to check out Commandos Paintball Club. Another popular club for go-karting enthusiasts, besides Formula-Kart, is Crazy Kart.

Those wishing to relax from an active pastime must visit the best spas in town. These include luxury Lotus Spa Health & Beauty Center and clean and tidy Aquaterra Wellness & Spa. Another place to enjoy a relaxing time is Megapolis, a swimming complex known for its cleanliness. Besides the aforementioned ones, the capital of Moldova has no less interesting bars to have a good time after nightfall. For example, this can be done in Pub Crawl, the atmosphere of which fun contributes to raising the mood, or in Deja Vu Bar where one can dance to the hottest hits. Karaoke bars are especially popular among tourists and locals alike, and Eli-Pili can be called one of the most popular bars in town.

So, Karaoke fans will enjoy a nice high quality karaoke nights in the most modern karaoke clubs in Chisinau such as: Art Club Karaoke, Black Chocolate karaoke Club, GAZ Karaoke and Night Club, Karaoke Club UpTown, Karaoke Concert Hall Atrium, MuzzCafe Karaoke, Karaoke Café Crocus, Pink Martini, Voice Vocal Club and many many others. You can choose to send a night in a karaoke club either if you like singing or not because it is a lot of fun having a great cocktail, enjoy others singing and even dancing and you can relax with friends and enjoy specialty treats. The Boulevard club is also known for an abundance of treats and fun parties; several times a week there are performances of popular DJs. Fans of contemporary music and dance would like a Dance Planet nightclub. Here is everything you need for a comfortable stay, including a large dance floor and perfectly matched music program, a cosy bar with an abundance of signature cocktails and a lounge with sofas, where you can take a break from dancing. Speaking about night clubs there are many, depending on what music you like and how much you want to spend; you can try Flamingo night Club, Fanconi, Rai Club, Cocos, Activ, Decadence, Piano Bar, Sky Bar and others. But keep in mind that there is face control in almost each night club and karaoke so you have to be dressed decent. Most probably if you are wearing shorts and trainers you will not be allowed to get in.

Gamblers will certainly be happy to visit one of the facilities where they can try their luck. Thus, Nuovo Casino attracts connoisseurs of luxury interiors and fine cuisine. Here there is an opportunity to play various types of poker, blackjack, American roulette. The classic interior of the best European casinos is recreated in Europa Casino. It presents the same games as in the facility described above, as well as the opportunity to put a bet for the dealer. Napoleon Palace Casino is the largest casino in the capital of Moldova. Players are provided with free meals, and the selection of games makes any gambler happy. Bowling Plaza with its lovely bar offering great drinks is waiting for those who want to hit some pins.

7. Accommodations in Chisinau, Apartments, Hotels:

Moldovans like to invest a lot in their houses; they do it great because they have good taste and they love to control every cm of job done in their house, they put also great accent on the quality, comfort and the atmosphere. And you will notice this either if you choose to stay in a hotel or in an apartment. Of course in order to find and book a place to stay it is better to use official sites and not particular persons. So you can start with: www.booking.com; www.airbnb.com; www. tripadvisor.com; have a look also here: www.chisinau-apartments.com .

If you are interested in staying in a hotel here you will find the best hotels in town their addresses and contact information: www. hotels.md

8. Public Transportation, Trolleybuses, Taxis, Cars rentals :

In Moldova there is only one airport and it is in Chisinau the capital of Moldova. If you come by plane and you didn't rent a car, it means you will be looking for ways to get to your hotel or apartment, there are a lot of suggestions: First, don't be afraid to use public transport in Moldova if you don't have big luggage you can choose to get to the center by trolley bus N 30 which will cost you 2 lei or by minibus N165 and it will cost you 3 lei. The minibuses are white vans leaving from the airport parking lot. If you leave the airport building from the arrivals area, turn right and walk towards the end of the building. The buses are marked with the number 165 on a sign behind the windshield and you can flag one down passing you, or walk up to the ones still parking. Don't open the sliding door even though you have luggage; they always use the co-drivers door to get on and off, but if you are tired and in a hurry of course you can take a taxi. There are three taxi companies which operate at the airport. The fixed fares range from about 80 to 120 MDL depending on which sector of the city you are going. There is a taxi stand at the airport offering fixed rates, the lady running the stand speaks English. Note that the rates posted are only a general suggestion, and you pay the metered fare to the driver. The fare should be no more than 120 lei to any destination in Chisinau. Do not take a particular taxi driver this will cost you double.

There are 40 taxi services operating throughout the city and its suburbs. Call 14222, 14333, 14444, 14747, 14448 or other 14xxx numbers to get a taxi. The easiest way to get a car is to install the application "Itaxi". If you don't have that possibility it is recommended to have a local person/hotel or restaurant call your taxi, as few Taxi drivers speak proper English. In case you need a receipt for your travel, you need to ask for this specifically when ordering. Also payment by credit card is impossible.

As of Jun 2018 all taxis charge by meter, so there is no need in negotiation. Many are using "electronic meters" in form of cell phone application, which cannot produce printed receipts.

Please remember to bring small bills, as sometimes they will not be "able" to give back on anything larger than 50 bills, but this is rare. Average prices vary across company/individual taxi driver, and it is fairly inconsistent. Expect prices between 30-60 for shorter rides and 50-150 Lei for longer rides.

Pay good attention to the traffic as a pedestrian, as the driving skills are rather poor combined with the fact that no one really follows normal traffic laws. Accidents are often occurring, and pedestrians should be very careful in terms of crossing streets.

Of course for the tourists the most comfortable and fast way to get somewhere is to take a taxi, but if you are adventurous and are looking for some new experience then you should use public transportation. It is comfortable and easy to take the trolleybus you just need to know the stop where to get off. The tickets are sold by the conductor walking up and down the trolleybus after each stop – it costs 2 lei. Do not expect any driver or conductor in the public transport to speak any English. The stops are announced only in some trolleybuses, so you either need to know where you are going by looks, or have a GPS map which would show you're nearby. If you choose to take the minibus you should know the number that will get you to your destination, it is not necessary to go to the bus station to get it Flag him down with your hand (just like you would with a taxi) when the vehicle approaches you on the street and it is usually OK to just tell the driver when you want to get off. Maxitaxi (rutierele) cost 3 lei, which is paid to the driver upon entry.

There is also the possibility to Rent a car and there are a lot of companies offering this service you just need to compare prices and conditions. In order to simplify your search here is a list of companies you can trust and rent a car:

www.rentalcars.com

http://motomix.md/en/lease

https://www.europcar.com/

www.4rent.md

www.sixt.com

Driving on Chisinau streets you have to be very careful as there are a lot of young drivers that do not respect the traffic rules and love the speed. In general roads in Moldova are not very good, some portions were renovated but some are really disastrous that is mainly in the countryside.

In Chisinau there are 3 main bus stations in order to travel outside Chisinau to other parts of the country. There is Central bus station which is located near the central market; from here all the busses go to the central part of Moldova but also abroad to Romania. North bus station – from here all the busses and mini buses go in the North direction of the country. And South bus station which is located on the outskirts of the town. So if you decide to travel the country by bus (and not renting a car) you can do this, but you have to know where you want to go and which bus you need to take. You will get information at any bus station regarding the timetables and costs of the trip; you can buy your ticket right there in the bus station before getting into the bus. There is the possibility to pay right to the driver although this is not desirable, in order to feel more confident and having you place in the bus, you better buy the ticket in the bus station.

This chapter was about Chisinau, and about some nice places to see, to eat and spend quality time with friends, family and even alone, but there are a lot of other places worth visiting while in Moldova, and we will speak about this in the next chapter.

THE WINE COUNTRY

Enjoy the genuine simplicity of life in rural Moldova and experience its true character. Moldova is a pastoral country with fertile soils and a benign and sunny climate. Vineyards dominate the landscape, but many other crops flourish here as well.

Village life has changed little in generations, traditional farming practices and ancient customs still keep pace with the changing seasons. Hors drawn carts make up much of the rural traffic and farm workers still gather in the evenings for traditional meals cooked outdoors.

For centuries Moldova has been distinguished as a country with hospitable people. The householders from the rural localities will be honoured to have you as a guest. The guests are usually invited in "Casa-Mare" a traditional room where all the family holidays are celebrated, being served at the same time with the most delicious and select dishes prepared in the rural household from the in-house ecological products.

The Legendary Wines of Moldova.

Moldovans have a passion for winemaking. Wines of Moldova are produced with care by talented winemakers from grapes that are mainly hand-picked from rich vineyards with local and international varieties expressing a unique, local taste. Moldovans award-winning wines have graced the tables of Russian Tzars and European Royalty for centuries. Because wine making is an important part of Moldovan tradition and culture, Moldova has a lot to offer for wine tourists.

While in Moldova you have to visit the vineyards, wineries and underground wine galleries that host the largest wine collections in the world, and take the time to taste some of the world's finest wines.

For centuries, Moldova has gained rich grape-growing and wine making traditions. Traditionally, the wine, which is also called "Lord's Blood" is served at different important events in the life of the Moldovans: christening, wedding, funerals and the most important Christian holidays such as Christmas, Easter and village/town celebrations.

Moldova offers tourists the chance to take various vine routes and visit cellars and underground cities, vinoteques, primary wine processing factories, enterprises producing sparkling wine, brandy, divin, balsams, etc.

.   .   .

Wineries and Wine Cellars:

According to the Moldovan tradition every householder must have a cellar to keep the wine he makes each autumn. Being a nation with patriarchal origins, for Moldovans the house has an important value. Moldovan's houses are composed of two basic elements – "casa mare" the room where the guests are received and the cellar where the food and wine is stored.

Traditionally peasants' cellars are dug at 5-7 meters depth under on or near the house having 10-15 stairs and the walls are whitewashed. It is a truly delight to taste a homemade eco wine in a cellar with a Moldovan peasant.

If you don't get the chance to see an authentic traditional cellar, you'll always have the possibility to visit the best Moldovan wineries:

Cricova Winery

Cricova - was founded in 1952 and is a unique underground complex located 12 km far from Chisinau, known worldwide due to its huge labyrinths, exceeding 120 km in length, and especially for its excellent wines. Cricova is one of the most important tourist attractions in Moldova. The jewel of the underground treasure is the National Vinoteque, which has a remarkable collection of over 600 of wine and brands from Italy, Spain, Portugal, France etc. The unique exhibits ("Jerusalem of Easter" vintage 1902, the liqueur "Jan Becher" vintage 1902) together with other 158 brands from Burgundy, Moselle, Tokay, the Rhine, are in the collection of the establishment as well as of Moldova in general, comprising nowadays a total of about 1.3 million bottles. Among those are the trophies of the Second World War, which include wines from the collection of Hermann Göring. After the Soviets seized his private wine collection, a part of it was transferred to

Crimea and the rest was brought to Cricova. Moldova only Cricova cellars employs the strict classic French technology of champagne wine production. So Cricova is a highlight of any visit to Moldova.

https://cricova.md/en/

Milestii Mici Winery

Milestii Mici was founded in 1969, it is located 20 km far from Chisinau in the locality of the same name of Ialoveni district.

This underground wine city appeared after the extraction of limestone deposits in the '70s of the last century, at a depth of 48-85m and is one of the largest in the world. The company became famous for its Golden Collection Wines. It was included in the Guiness Book of Records as the largest wine collection in Europe, with over 1,5 million collection bottles. The total number of bottles stored in the cellars of Milestii Mici exceeds 2 million. The complex of galleries from Milestii Mici is the largest in Europe, stretching over nearly 250 km are used and may be travelled through by vehicle. The wines stored here are made of different harvest years between 1968 and 1991.

https://www.milestii-mici.md/en/

Purcari Winery

Purcari Winery is the oldest winery in Moldova being founded in 1827. It is located in Purcari Village, Stefan Voda district, which is situated 130 km far from Chisinau. It has a rich historical heritage producing some of the most genuine Moldovan Wines: "Negru de Purcari" and "Rosu de Purcari" – a must try.

After two decades, Purcari wines, but first the famous brand "Negru de

Purcari" became popular and entered the European market. And in 1878, at the World's Fair held in Paris, the wine "Negru de Purcari" won the first gold medal, beating the famous wines of Bordeaux. Purcari wines were ordered to be served at their tables by Russian Emperor Nicolas II, King of the United Kingdom George V, and Queen of the United Kingdom Victoria.

https://purcari.wine/en/

Chateau Vartely Winery:

Chateau Varteley winery from Orhei town was funded in 2008 and is located 48 km from Chisinau. The factory specializes in producing quality wines with full cycle: beginning with the growing of vines on their own vineyards and ending with the quality brut wines production and bottling. Within the factory a modern tourist complex operates. The complex has a special architecture and represents a true landscape delight, situated on a hill from a breathtaking view opens. The court full of wine museum items, reminds the perfect blend of architectural art with wine art. In the middle of limestone rock, in Chateau Vartely collection rooms, the visitors have the perfect conditions for a true tasting with the ideal temperature and humidity.

https://www.vartely.md/en

Branesti Cellars Winery:

Branesti Cellars Winery was founded in 1996 in Branesti Village, Orhei district and is located 48 km far from Chisinau. The factory covers a distance of 58 km at a depth of 60m below ground and has an area of 75 ha. The factory has two tasting rooms with impressive architecture, one of which is located in the underground. They are made of wood and metal and reproduce images related to wine cultivation and wine production. Here the guests are able to enjoy white and red collection wines, sparkling wines, traditional dishes prepared by skilled cooks and the water Poiana Branesti bottled at a depth of 75 m below ground.

Migdal-P Wine company:

Migdal-P Wine company was founded on 21 September 1995 and the first bottling wines were put in operation in December 1999. The company is located in the heart of Codri, in Cojusna village, 18 km from Chisinau and includes the famous "Chateau Cojusna". The vineyards with the vines of the company cover about 400 ha and the cultivated varieties are: Merlot, Pinot Noir, Chardonnay, Cabernet.

Inside the cellar there are 3 tasting rooms, wine aging hall and collection wines gallery. In the tasting rooms with heavy oak chairs and walls build with secular stone, valuable collection wines can be enjoyed.

Mimi Castle Winery:

Mimi Castle Winery is just 35 km far from Chisinau, and it is the first wine Chateau of Moldova. It was founded in 1893, by the last Governor of Bessarabia, Constantin Mimi (1868-1953). Mimi Castle was during the 20th century the glory of Moldovan wines. The history of the Castle as the history of Bessarabia, has known 3 crucial periods: the tsarist domination, the unification with Romania and the Independence of Republic of Moldova.

In 2010 the restoration of the Castle started, and stone by stone in 5 years it was restored to its initial state. The Mimi Castle is an attraction for tourists from all over the world. The architecture of the Castle was inspired from France. Constantin Mimi studied viticulture at the

Superior School of Agronomy from Montpellier. The cellars of the Castle are unique in Moldova and they keep a constant temperature of 13 degrees all year long.

Spread over an area of 5 hectares, Mimi Castle includes a hotel and a restaurant, underground cellars, tasting rooms, a wine shop, an art gallery, a museum and also the winery and the vineyard which are among the most important elements of the castle. The vineyard of 35 ha is only 2 km far from the Dniester River.

https://www.castelmimi.md/en_index.html

Asconi Winery:

The company Asconi was founded in 1994. The winery was developed based on modern winemaking technologies, while winemakers of the company have used the most advanced production facilities. Asconi today owns about 600 hectares of vineyards, located at a distance of only 8-10 km from the winery. European varieties are cultivated, but special attention is given to indigenous varieties such as Rară Neagră, Feteasca Regală (Moldovan), Saperavi (Georgian) etc. One of the peculiarities of the Asconi winery is that they pick grapes mechanically at night, as the grapes are still cold. Asconi wines are not sold in Moldova, they are exported to EU countries, Chile, Brazil, Australia, USA, Israel, Africa etc. The only place where these wines can be purchased and tasted is the winery shop.

In 2014 winery opens its doors to visitors. The tourist complex presents two restaurant halls, a spacious terrace overlooking the courtyard of the winery. Here you can enjoy exclusive dishes of national cuisine, prepared in the oven according to original recipes. Tours are guided personally by one of the winemakers or company managers.

For excellence and outstanding performance, the Winery Asconi, receives in 2015 he the National Grand Prix of wine industry.

http://asconi.md/?lang=en

Et Cetera Winery:

Et Cetera produces unique wines with a flavor enriched with the spirit of Moldovan territory. Et Cetera cultivates relationships between humans and nature, homeland; cultivate interpersonal relations.

The menu of the restaurant features Et Cetera's house specialty dishes including homemade placinte, high quality meats and fish. All dishes are prepared exclusively from local organic products. Depending on weather conditions an outdoor seating can be arranged, on the terrace with beautiful views of the vineyards.

Each year, the winery is visited by guests from all around the world. They are hosted by the winemaker who organizes tastings right in the factory and the wines are tasted from barrels and tanks.

https://etcetera.md/

Kvint:

Kvint is a brandy distillery located in Tiraspol, the largest city in Transnistria. Kvint also produces vodka and wine. Founded in 1897, it is the oldest still-operating enterprise in the region. Initially, Kvint produced only vodka. It started to produce brandy in 1938.

Since then, Kvint has become well known in the region and around the world for its high-quality brandies, which it produces following classical French technologies. The brandies are aged in oak barrels for 3-50 years depending upon the product. Kvint offers daily guided tours and tastings that range in price depending upon the number samples served and the quality.

Bardar Winery:

In 1929 a German entrepreneur named Muller, laid the foundation of what is today Bardar Winery – a small distillery in the village Bardar not far away from Chisinau. Already in '40 this distillery was transformed into a veritable factory for the production of distillates and wines. Currently Bardar Winery is in top 3 cognac producers in Moldova. The company produces cognac, wine distillates ; aged 3 years, 5 years, 7 years, 10 years and 20 years. Unlike wine which can be considered a living organism until it is consumed, the distillates live only in a barrel. As the quality of wood and indoor humidity are fundamental for the final product.

Only grapes, oak and patience – these are the necessary ingredients to produce Bardar brandy, an exclusive and authentic wine distillate.

If you are a cognac lover then you have to try Bardar Platinul Collection, which has a rich and expressive bouquet, with notes of chocolate and resin.

When deciding to visit any of these wineries you can book on their official website, either you can choose some companies that organize tours: www.winetours.md; www.best-moldova.md they will make sure you'll have the most enjoyable tours you can imagine.

MONASTERIES

THE LANDSCAPES, CULTURAL AND TOURIST ATTRACTIONS, HISTORICAL vestiges, gastronomic traditions and the hospitality of the Moldovans, are attractive elements of rural and gastronomic tourism in Moldova.

The intangible cultural heritage which includes the folklore and customs, and the local crafts is highly leveraged within the rural tourism, offering visitors the opportunity to learn about the daily life of native rural people, the charm of holidays, to taste the traditional Moldovan cuisine based on local products, grown in ecological conditions, to enjoy horse and cart riding in summer, and sledge riding in winter, biking and hiking, tours to tourist attractions, cultural activities, etc.

The Moldovan cuisine is rich, delicious and stands out by a great variety of dishes, well cooked and interestingly served, with balanced spicing, depending on the specifics of the place.

Holy places as elements of cultural heritage are of particular interest to visitors, being included in various travel packages.

Currently about 1200 churches operate in Moldova, 81 of which are included in the list of monuments protected by the state, and 56 monasteries that are also part of the cultural heritage of the country.

Capriana Monastery:

Capriana Monastery dedicated to the "Assumption of Virgin Mary" is located in Capriana village, 36 km from Chisinau and 16 km from Straseni town, being one of the oldest monasteries of Bessarabia. The first documented reference of the church dates back in 1420. Having the status of monastery of the prince, several princes of Moldova took care of the monastic endowment. The monastery which was build at first of wood, suffered from the repeated invasions of the Tatars or Turks. Stefan the Great is the founder of the stone church dedicated to the "Assumption of the Virgin Mary" (1491-1496)

Curchi Monastery:

Curchi Monastery is one of the most important architectural monuments of Bessarabia, and it is also considered to be one of the most beautiful and famous monasteries of the region. It is dedicated to the "Nativity of Virgin Mary" and is located in Orhei forest near Curchi village, approximately 14 km southwest of the town of Orhei. The monastery is situated in the Vatici valley on a bank of the Vatic River between rich hills covered with forests, gardens and orchards. The monastery is a real gem, offering silence and peace.

The monastery has a rich religious and cultural past spanning more than two centuries. It was founded in 1773-1775 and became one of the richest, most beautiful, and largest monasteries in Moldova.

Several churches were build on the monastery's premises: St. Demetrius, a wooden church built in 1775 by Ioan Curchi; Naşterea Domnului, a stone church built in 1810; the winter church of St. Demetrius built in 1844; the summer church Naşterea Domnului built in 1872; and the winter church of St. Nicholas (unfinished), built in 1936-1939.

Monastery's main church, the cathedral Naşterea Domnului (1872), was built in baroque style, inspired by the church of St. Andrew in Kiev, which was designed by Italian architect Bartolomeo Rastrelli. The cathedral has the highest dome in Moldova, rising to a height of 57 meters.

During the World War II, a fire at the monastery destroyed the icons and gilded iconostasis inside the church. In addition, two of the four original belfries were destroyed. In 1943, the cathedral was repainted. Unfortunately, from 1959-1995 the monastery was used as a psychiatric hospital. During this time, some repairs were made in 1993, but it was largely neglected until 1999.

The monastery was reopened in 2005, but still badly in need of repair. Then in 2006, under the patronage of the former President of Moldova, a large fund-raising campaign, "Curchi Monastery: From Ruins to Elevation", was organized to support the restoration of the monastery. Today the monastery is undergoing a complete renovation.

.   .   .

Hancu Monastery:

The monastery is dedicated to "Pious Saint Paraskeva" and is situated in the forest about 70 km west from Chisinau, and it borders with Cogilnic river. The Hancu Monastery was built in the place of the hermitage of nuns in 1678 by the high steward Mihail Hancu in order to satisfy the will of one of his daughters who became a nun whose name was Parascheva. Until the 17th century the hermitage bore the name Viadica.

The legend says that Hâncu needed a big army in order to dethrone the voivode Gheorghe Ducas and he received help from his relative the cavalry commander apostle Durac, and from the clever Sorocean Constantin who followed to marry his daughter. Closer to the day of marriage his daughter refused to marry the ally of his father and she ran from the parental house and hid in a lair. The daughter of Mihalcea Hancu stayed a period of time in a cave and she was founded by the hunters who were looking for her. The girl refused to go with them. Then her father came personally and implored her to get out from the cave. She accepted but with the condition that she will get out when hearing the chime of church bells. Thus, Mihalcea Hancu ordered to be built a church where his daughter lived the rest of her life.

After the Tatar invasion in Moldova the church was destroyed and the afferent buildings the same, thus the hermitage being ruined completely.

In 1784 the prior of the monastery, Varlaam the second built some hermitages for frocking and a wood church.

In September 1949 the Hancu Monastery was closed and in 1992 after a period of 43 years when it was closed, the monastery resumed its activity.

. . .

Saharna Monastery:

The "Holy Trinity" Monastery of Saharna, situated about 110 km north of Chisinau on the right side of the Nistru, is considered to be one of the biggest centres for religious pilgrimages in Moldova. Here can be found the unique relics of St. Cuvios Macarie, and on the top of the high cliff, according to a legend, there is a footprint of St. Maria. The legend says that a monk from the monastery (X-XII c., documentary XVII-XVIII c.) once saw the shining figure of Saint Maria on the top of a rock. When reaching that spot the monk saw a mark of a footstep on the ground. This vision was considered to be a divine announcement and evidence of the holy purity of this place. Near this spot a new wooden church was built and the "Holy Trinity" monastery founded (1777). Later the wooden church was replaced by a brick one built in an old Moldavian style, decorated with frescos. Meanwhile the community of monks expanded. The monastery can be visited daily.

An exceptional panoramic view of the numerous rocky hills and the forests around the small 16-km river, which runs down 30 cascades and waterfalls, is opened up to the traveler from the cliff-tops. Here there is also an important archaeological site with the remains from the Iron Age (X-VIII c. BC) and a Geto-Dacian headland fortress (IV-III c. BC), which has been preserved in a better condition than any other in Moldova.

Tipova Monastery:

In Tipova on the rocky side of the Nistru river (about 100-km north of Chisinau), is the biggest Orthodox cave monastery in Moldova and in Eastern Europe. Long before the feudal state of Moldova was formed, a community of monks was established here. Some say that in the X-XII c. (according to others in the XVI-XVIII c.) some cells were dug inside the steep cliffs of the Nistru. In 1776 a prosperous period started when the monastery was divided into large parts, separated by massive columns. During the Soviet period the monastery was closed and destroyed. In 1975 the ruins of the Tipova monastery were protected by the State and in 1994 religious services resumed.

It is said that the wedding of our great Ruler Stefan cel Mare and his wife Maria Voichita was held in this monastery. Another legend says that the mythological poet Ortheus spent his last years on these hills and is buried in a nook of a waterfall. The monastery can be visited daily.

Tourists can visit the splendid path though the "Tipova" nature reserve. In ancient times (IV-III c. BC) a Geto-Dacian fortress stood in the grounds. Its remains are still visible.

Zabriceni Monastery:

Zabriceni Monastery dedicated to the "Nativity of our Lord" is located about 200 km north from Chisinau and 12 km from Edinet town. The monastic settlement is located at the edge of the forest in a very picturesque place. At the monastery all praises and Divine Liturgy are celebrated. The style typical to the monastery is Byzantine, following the model of the Mount Athos. Choir chant Psaltic-Byzantine.

Calaraseuca Monastery:

Calaraseuca Monastery dedicated to the "Assumption of Virgin Mary" is situated on the right bank of the Dniester River in Calaraseuca village, Ocnita district in the North of Moldova at a distance of about 210 km from Chisinau. Surrounded by the rocks and the old Dniester River, its history begins with 1648. Those who come to the monastery can see the scenery of the landscape reserve "Calaraseuca" located near the holy sanctuary.

Dobrusa Monastery:

Dobrusa monastery dedicated to "Saint Nicolas the Great Holy Hierarch", is located 127 km. north from Chisinau. It is situated between the hills covered with woods and surrounded by orchards. According to some sources the monastery was founded in 1772 by a monk Ioasaf who came from the monastery Probota, Suceava.

Hirjeuca Monastery:

It is situated 70 km. north-west of Chisinau. The community of monks appeared in this area for the first time in 1740. Later some wooden churches and cells were built. The first half of the XIX c. was a flourishing period for the Hirjeuca Convent. It was surrounded by lakes, fountains and paths in a well designed park. In 1836 the summer "Resurrection" church was built in a similar classic architectural style as the Cathedral of Chisinau. Later came the winter church, "St. Spiridon". In 1922 the interior of the latter is painted by the famous painter Pavel Piscarev. Hirjeuca Convent had an impressive library and a school for children of clerics. During the Soviet period the convent was closed, and functioned instead as a sanatorium. In 1993 the convent was reopened. In its grounds one can find the famous "Spring of Youth" which has curative properties. Visitors can make an excursion through the local forest, which is considered to be a valuable natural monument.

The Convent can be visited daily.

· · ·

Japca Monastery:

The Japca Monastery is situated on the shore of Dniestr (Nistru) River at the distance of 10 km from Camenca. It is the only monastery from Bessarabia which was never closed by the Soviet authorities.

The Japca area (160 km north the Chisinau) is very well known for its convent of nuns, the only one to remain open during the Soviet period. In XVIIth c. the convent community was similar to a fortress. The first recorded date of the hermitage goes back to 1693, when the monks lived in the inside cells and held religious services in the church, which was also inside caves. In 1770 the monks moved out to the current monastery. It was a period of a new construction style and increasing wealth. A rich library was founded too. At the beginning of the XIXth c. stone churches were built as well. The most important church of the convent was frequently rebuilt, thus now having three altars: Resurrection, Transfiguration, Crucifixion. Visitors are very impressed by the traditions that still prevail within the community. The convent can be daily visited.

Other interesting sightseeing opportunities include the Geo-paleonthological monument "Japca Rock", a mineral water spring, Rascov landscape nature reserve and palaeolithic sites at Socola and Rascov. In Camenca town is the "Nistru" sanatorium.

Next to the interesting sightseeing of this place there is the Geo-paleonthological monument "Japca Rock", a mineral water spring, landscape reservoir Rascov and paleolitical stations at Socola and Rascov. In Camenca town sanatorium "Nistru" is functioning.

Rudi Monastery:

Situated about 200km north of Chisinau, Rudi is one of the most interesting places to visit. One can find here pre-historic remains in a natural, 100m long cave, also an exceptional nature reserve, an ancient headland fortress (IV-III c. BC), two ring-shaped fortresses (IX-XII c.) called "Turkish Plate" and "Germanariu", and a rural community rich in traditions. But the main object of visit in this area is one of the oldest monasteries in Moldova. The monastery has preserved the traditional monks' way of life through the centuries and the "Holy Trinity" church built in 1777 is considered to be a representative sample of the old Moldavian religious architectural style. The church is situated in a beautiful natural setting in the valley of river Bulboana.

The monastery can be visited daily.

Frumoasa Monastery:

The beautiful monastery dedicated to the "Holy Trinity", is located 65 km northwest from Chisinau. It is situated o a sloping hill surrounded on all sides by wooden hills and open view to the south, from where we can see the beautiful slopes with groves and lush gardens from the Ichel River Valley. In autumn 1804 three hieromonks, who came from the Neamtu monastery to Raciula skete, agreed to establish a monastery in Frumusica glade.

Noul Neamt Monastery:

Noul Neamț is an all-male monastery located in Chițcani, near Tighina, geographically in Basarabia but controlled by the breakaway Transnistrian authorities. It is also known as Mănastirea Chițcani, and it is the biggest religious complex under the control of Transnistrian authorities.

The monastery of the Holy Ascension in New-Neamts is situated in Basarabia, on the right shore of Dniester, at a distance of 14 km from the town of Tighina (Bender) and 6 km from the town of Tiraspol. The monastic complex rises grandly to the sky, being seen from the distance by the people coming near the village of Chitcani.

There are four churches on the territory of the monastery. In the center, the wonderful Ascension cathedral is situated. On its left there is the old church built in the honour of the Saint Hierarch Nicholas the Wonder-Worker. Opposite there is a refectory church, of the Ascension of the Holy Cross. The Dormition church is a congruous part with its five chapels completing the general view of the monastery.

The name (which means "New Neamț" in English) signifies that the monastery is a successor of the Neamț Monastery in Romania (medieval Moldavia).

The monastery was founded in 1861, when several monks from the Neamț monastery left and founded Noul-Neamț in Chițcani. The founding of the new monastery was a protest against the measures taken in United Principalities of Romania to confiscate monastery estates and forbid the usage of Slavonic language in worship.

On 16 May 1962 Soviet authorities closed the monastery; the buildings became a hospital.

The monastery church was reopened in 1989, followed in 1991 by the Romanian-language school for Orthodox priests.

Even if Moldova is not a big country, it has been blessed with various unique landscapes, natural monuments of international value, and places filled with the charm of nature.

Padurea Domneasca:

The scientific reserve Padurea Domneasca (Royal Forest) is a protected area in Moldova, it was founded in 1993 and covers an area of about 6,032 ha. Geographically it is located **185 km** far from Chisinau city, in the Prut River bottomland, on the territory of the forest farms of Glodeni and Falesti districts. It is unique by its biodiversity, including one of the oldest forests in the Prut River bottomland and one of the oldest bottomland forests in Europe. The flora of the reserve is rich and diverse. Over 700 species of local flora out of the 1,300 registered in the country can be found here. The bisons represent the pride of the reserve.

"Codrii" Natural Reserve:

Codrii" Reserve was created on **27 September 1971** in the central area of the Republic of Moldova based on the forest range Lozova, Straseni district, about **45 km** far from Chisinau city, with the purpose of preserving the most representative sectors of forests typical of the Central Plateau of the country. The total area of the reserve is 17,476 ha. The flora is represented by 1,000 species of plants, and the fauna comprises about 52 species of mammals, 151 species of birds,8 species of reptilians,10 species of amphibians and over 8,000 species of insects. While visiting Codrii you can stop for a lunch at the traditional restaurant " Doi Haiduci" where they serve delicious zeama and other Moldavian dishes. You can even stay for the night because there are small houses that you can rent in order to enjoy the silence and fresh air in the middle of the mother nature.

"Prutul de Jos" Natural Reserve:

"Prutul de Jos" Reserve was created in April 1991 and it is located in the south-western part of the Republic of Moldova along the lower course of the Prut River, the last great tributary of the Danube River at the border between Romania and the Republic of Moldova. The total area of the reserve is 1,691 ha. The reserve situated about 200km far from Chisinau between the villages Valeni and Slobozia Mare, in Cahul district. The main geographical component of the reserve is the Beleu lake that has an area of 628 ha.

It was discovered that Prut bottomland represents an important migration route, and the water basins with rush-beds, willow forests, etc. represent an appropriate place for having a rest, feeding and nestling for many species of birds. For a period of some years 189 species of birds, 34 species of mammals,7 species of reptilians,11 species of fish were registered in the reserve.

.   .   .

"Plaiul Fagului" Natural Reserve:

One of the state reserves where the natural ecosystems with a less human influence were preserved is "Plaiul Fagului" Reserve. The reserve was created in **March 1992, 75 km** far from Chisinau city, and covers an area of 5,642 ha, including 5,375 ha with forests. The fauna is represented by 211 species. Nowadays, on the territory of the reserve there are very often found the red deer.

"Iagorlic" Natural Reserve:

"Iagorlic" Reserve was founded in February 1988. It is located on the left bank of the Dniester River, at the entry of Iagorlic River, near Goieni bight. The territory of the reserve covers an area of 836 ha of dry land and 270 ha of water.

The flora is represented by 719 species of plants found in the reserve, of which 50 species are rare. The fauna of the reserve is composed by 167 species of birds, of which 15 species are included in the Red Book of the Republic of Moldova,29 species of mammals and 23 species of fish.

6. Landscape Reserves:

The Landscape Reserves represent a part of the natural heritage of the country, being created in order to protect and preserve the biodiversity of the Republic of Moldova.

Landscape reserve "Toltrele Prutului:

In the northwestern part of the Republic of Moldova there are places with quite spectacular landscapes. The small rivers, tributaries from the left side of the Prut River, dig deep canyons through the cliffs covered with moss. These are old reefs formed by hard limestone where high concentrations of remnants of various organisms can be noticed such as: marine algae of specific form, corals, sea urchins, scallops and other marine animals that used to live in the tropical Tortonian and Sarmatian seas 10-2- million years ago. These reefs form the landscape reserve "Toltrele Prutului"(or Reefs of Prut) that are a chain of limestone formations of reef type, situated in Moldova, alongside Middle Prut, on a distance of about 200 km.

Landscapes reserve "The Hundred Knolls":

The landscape reserve "The Hundred Knolls" is situated in the Prut bottomland, about 205 km north of Chisinau city, between Braniste village, Riscani district, and Cobani village, Glodeni district. This name is inappropriate as in reality the number is bigger-over 3,500 knolls, covering an area of 1,072 ha. Their height varies from 1.5 to 30.5. Some scientists consider that "The Hundred Knolls" is the only place in Europe where there are concentrated in such a great number the submarine reefs of the Mediterranean Sea-tertiary water basin, that covered about 20 million years ago the current territory of the Republic of Moldova.

The reserve has a special scientific value not only from the geological point of view, but also from the floristic and faunistic ones.

7. "Orheiul Vechi"- an open air museum:

Archaeologists have discovered many remains of ancient towns and villages on the territory of Moldova, but the place called Orheiul Vechi is no doubt the most famous and has particular historical significance. In addition, the beauty of the landscape is extraordinary at sunrise, just as at dusk, when the rocky shore of Răut takes unusual shapes and colours.

Orheiul Vechi was recently registered on the list of UNESCO due to its historical value. It is the most iconic place in Moldova. It holds the most wonderful views of the hills and caves, including a monastery in a cave as well as beautiful views over the Butuceni and Trebuieni villages. It is considered to be one of most powerful energetic places in the country with plenty of space for hiking and discovering the national heritage. If you wish to have a different experience, a different view over this country, then this place is a MUST to visit and it is only 45 km's away from Chisinau.

Let's have a look at the history of this place. For thousands of years Moldova has been conquered by different tribes and empires and this settlement actually contains some of the archaeological remains of those times. Between the XIII – XIV century this area was under the control of Tatar-Mongols during the Golden Hoard. The original settlement was destroyed and rebuild in oriental style having a mosque and public baths. Until nowadays you can see the remains of the baths and mosque.

After a while Moldovans have gained the power and kicked out the Golden Hoart, but later on the Tatars came back to conquer the territory. Moldovans have managed to strengthen it with a fortress, plenty of churches, houses and defence structures which helped them stand their ground and become one of the most important defence spots in the country. Defeated, the Tatars never came back to reclaim this land.

Nowadays, the Monastery cave is well known for its legend and for its placement. It is said that the ruler of the Golden Hoard hid his golden cart and all his treasure and gold in the walls of rocks when he found out that they were under attack and are going to lose.

It was not only a place for hiding gold, but also for hiding pilgrims and orthodox Christians during the Soviet Union period. As religion was forbidden, many followers and monks used this place as their sacred space. Today it is still a church which is used by locals for praying. It is also an attractive place for visiting for locals and for foreigners. There is a new church built nearby where all the religious services take place. If you wish to attend the service in the main church, you can do it daily from 7am to 5pm.

Another interesting fact to mention about Orheiul Vechi is that over 30 million years ago this region was the bottom of the "Sarmatic" Sea which stretched all the way to Central Asia. You can the proof of this just by looking at the rock and walls in this area – sea shells. Even in the cave monastery when looking around you will see that there are many sea shells in the walls.

Not far from the cave monastery there is a cross with the "Flower of Life" symbol on it, which is considered to make your wishes come true just by putting your hand on it, that is why there may be a queue of tourists and even local people.

8. Eco Resort Butuceni:

If going from historical - religious to traditional but remaining also in Orheiul Vechi, down the hill on the right side is the Butuceni village called nowadays Eco Resort Butuceni. It is a place that boasts traditional Moldovan style houses and village life. At the entrance of the village there is a tourist information point for those that need info about the area, including public transport timetable. There is also a village museum which you can visit to discover how traditional Moldovan houses looked inside and what the life in the area was and still is like. The entrance to the museum is 10 lei that is 50 cents. For those seeking to experience the most authentic village life they can communicate with locals as some of the; sell their home made products – wine, pies, honey.

If speaking about food, there are few places to try out if you are ready to taste some authentic Moldovan food. There are two main restaurants: "Eco Butuceni Resort" and "Villa Etnica" which provide traditional Moldovan cuisine and wine. Also nearby there are a few more options, including airbnb's which provide lodging in case you decide to stay for the night. In these houses food is cooked on a wood burning stove and people sleep on a "lejanca" (sunbed). The pies, the marmalade, the sarmale (stuffed cabbage) and the pickles are the specialty of the houses, being served in a room decorated with Moldovan carpets, basil and a real carpet weaving machine. Here you will taste fresh fruit and vegetables from the guesthouses gardens. The peasant farm with delight you, and you will be provided with a carriage for trips through the village. On the narrow streets of Butuceni you can see children running barefoot or peasants riding,and you can also stop at fountains with fresh and cool water.At the same time,modernism has slowly slipped in here,the pansion was given three stars,being connected who all utilities,having even a Spa center and an inside pool. On certain occasions you can catch a little concert with Moldovan folk music.

Some other things this place is famous for: paragliding and parachute jumping, as well as for hosting music festivals such as "Gustar" which takes place every year in August and DescOpera – Open Air Opera.

http://www.pensiuneabutuceni.md/en/home

If you plan to visit Orheiul Vechi you have a few transport options. There is a mini bus which goes daily from the central bus station in Chisinau to Butuceni at the following times: 10:20/15:00/18:15. Pay attention, do not take the Orhei min bus as that one goes to the Orhei city, which is not old Orhei area. Other options which will make you take out some money of your pocket are: take a taxi which will coast you around 50 euros per day, rent a car or book a tour. It is for you to decide but when in Moldova, it is highly recommended to visit these places.

The Guest House "Casa de sub Stinca"

The guesthouse "Casa de sub Stinca" is located in Trebujeni Village, in the heart of the archeological complex "Orheiul Vechi" . (Old Ohei) The guesthouse is the 11th house from the beginning of the village, located right under a rock, causing great interest among visitors.

"Casa de sub Stinca" will offer you accommodation in renovated rooms, decorated in a traditional Moldovan style with own access to the bath room.

Also here you will enjoy the traditional Moldovan food prepared by the hostess from local ingredients.

Here you can spend unforgettable holidays in a village atmosphere with traditional dishes and a lot of good mood.

Guest House "Casa Parinteasca"

The guest house "Casa Părintească" (Parents' House) is located in the village of Palanca, Calarasi region and is a real museum of rural life. The owner, Mrs Tatiana Popa, has turned the family home into a museum of crafts. The museum displays artefacts of traditional peasant life, including old textiles, household items, tools, photographs and a jumble of fabrics, stitchery and weaving. Visitors have the chance to learn about a unique technique of carpet weaving, called "covorul in bumbi". A forgotten tradition, but revived by the Casa Parintească. These handicrafts have served as inspiration for famous designers in Europe. A famous designer Isabell de Hillerin, being impressed by the beauty of the elements that create this work of art, decided to use it in the "haute couture". Even the famous French company Chanel arrived to the Casa Parintească in search of inspiration and originality. Some handicrafts are available for purchase. For large groups, depending on weather conditions can be arranged an ethno-folk program with traditional songs and dances.

Lunch is usually served in the museum courtyard. The menu includes traditional meals paired with homemade wine. You can also possible to taste bio herbal tea, the cherry compote and rose liqueur, both with outbreaking flavour.

Next to the museum it is a splendid old wooden church – Holy Virgin Protection. The church was built of larch wood from Ukraine at the end of the eighteenth century.

9. Soroca Fortress:

In the medieval period the **fortress of Soroca** was part of a huge Moldovan defensive system, which comprised four fortresses on the Nistru river, two on the Danube and another three in the northern part of the country. With this "stone belt of fortresses", the country borders were well protected. Soroca fortress was built at the Nistru river crossing, on older fortifications. In 1499, on the order of Stefan cel Mare, a square wooden fortress was built, on the site of a former Genovan fortress called as Olihonia (Alciona).

Between 1543–1546, while Petru Rares ruled the country, the fortress was completely re-built in stone, and in the shape that you can see it today – a perfect circle, the diameter of which is 37,5 m and with 5 bastions situated at equal distances. When designing the fortress the builders incorporated the supreme law of harmony "the golden section", which makes the fortress unique among examples of European defensive architecture.

Soroca's fortress is also famous for being the place where the Moldovan army, commanded by the famous statesman Dimitrie Cantemir, and the Russian army, led by the Tsar Petru I, met and consolidated their forces during the Prut campaign against the Turkish hordes in 1711. Along history, the fortress has been visited by Bogdan Hmelnitski, Timush Hmelnitski, Alexander Suvorov, and others. The fortress is the only medieval monument in Moldova, which has been preserved entirely as it was designed by its builders. Above the entrance gate you can visit the small military church.

10. "Luminarea Recunostintei"Monument:

While in Soroca and after visiting the fortress and buying souvenirs in the boutiques that you will see next to the fortress there is one more place you have to visit– Luminarea Recunostintei monument (**The Candle of Gratitude Monument) it** is one of the best monuments in Moldova. The monument is built on the rocks over the Nistru River. It is also considered as a very special work of art for another reason. It is actually built in the memory of the cultural monuments in Moldova that were destroyed in the past. It is a silent witness of many hopes and agonies, dreams and hard works of many past generations.

The Candle of Gratitude Monument pays homage to all the heroes of the country who always worked to preserve the culture and tradition of Moldova. They did not just secure their culture but also showcased the true colours of Moldavian tradition and history before the world. In another way round, the monument as well as these safeguards of Moldavian tradition paid a tribute to the forefather of their literature; the anonymous writer of the poem "Miorita".

This national monument was the brain child of a famous Moldavian classical writer Ion Druta. This man always had a deep respect for the tradition and culture of Moldova. He wanted to pay homage to their ancestors who worked so hard to preserve the Moldavian culture. The idea of making a monument came to his mind some twenty years ago but the project was inaugurated only on March 27th, 2004. The Moldavian people contributed in various manners to complete this project. Some contributed with work, some helped by taking care of the finance. It shows the love and respect the Moldavians have for their country. On this top there appears a candle-shaped chapel 29,5 meters long, which during the night time has a light which goes as far as Otaci and Camenca. You can admire a magnificent indescribable view from the top of this hill. The tour to Moldova remains incomplete if this national monument is not visited.

11. Tighina Fortress:

Tighina fortress is located on the bank of the Dniester River. It was one of the most powerful fortresses of Moldova.

During the '70-'80 of the 14th century, Tighina was incorporated to the Principality of Moldova. Tighina becomes an important point on the Moldovan Trade Route linking Western Europe with Orient through the Danube ford from Isaccea, Byzantine regions from the right of the Danube with Caffa, Genoese colony in the Crimea. This trade route was also called Tartar Road. This road crossed in Tighina with the fluvial road leading from Hotin to Soroca, White Fortress and the Black Sea.

At the end of the 15th century, near the old locality Tighina, a fortress of wood and earth was built, thus completing the defense system of medieval Moldova and being in those times one of the most powerful citadels. The fortress was meant to impede the entry to Moldova, though the pass from Tighina, of the Tatars who participated in the Ottoman campaigns of 1476 and 1484 Ottoman against Stefan the Great.

After the defeat in Poltava(1709),the Swedish King Charles XII took refuge for several years in Bender.

ALTERNATIVE ACTIVITIES

Moldova is known as a wine country and its tourism is mainly based on it. But there are plenty of other things to do here besides wine tasting and sightseeing, how about some activities which require more physical movement? For those seeking for adventures or a different way to discover this country here is a list of alternative activities in Moldova.

Hiking:

If you are interested in trips out of Chisinau, if you want to explore the local nature put your body at work then hiking is the best option for you. There are a couple of people that offer such experience for a fee in various beautiful points of the country. You can find their pages on Facebook and even if their main conversational languages are Romanian and Russian, they are providing information in English as well, so feel free to contact them if you feel it. The most famous local hiking trips are organised by Outdoor Moldova and by High and Low Adventures, set up on specific dates. (see their facebook pages). Hiking

Moldova are very English friendly, Alex Hoinaru offers hiking experiences in Pohreabna village and nearby.

Vespa Tours:

I am sure you did not expect to find a Vespa in Moldova, but die to the lovers of these little gems a unique idea has popped up – Vespa Tours in Moldova. You can Enjoy a tour on a Vespa in Chisinau but also outside the city, to Orheiul Vechi or even much further to the South and to the North. Some of these tours can be customised, including overnight camping stays. Besides tours they also rent their Vespas for photo shoots, videos or just a couple of hours to discover the city by yourself. For more specific information you can contact them on their Facebook business page Vespa Moldova.

Kayaking:

For those who love spending time on the water, kayaking would be an interesting option. In Moldova there are two main companies that offer this activity organised as tours with guides or self guided. Kayaking.md are mostly concentrated on Russian speakers offering day trips along Nistru river (Dniester), but also kayaking trips abroad. Their options are more suitable for groups as they require that they have at least 6 canoes for a trip. Another options which is English friendly is the kayakingtours.md, offering a variety of daily guided and self guided tours. They are situated in Vadul lui Voda and provide trips to the South and to the North of Moldova on Nistru, Prut and in Danube Delta form the 1st of April until the 30th of October. Besides canoe they also provide bicycles and camping gear. Children get in for free if both of the parents are present and they require at least 2 people per booking. In order to find out more information and they contact details feel free to visit their website indicated above.

. . .

Ural Tours:

If you are looking to experience some of the soviet vibes and impress your friends with craxy ideas of just for curiosity, Ural tours provides a great opportunity – tours on the legendary Russian sidecar motorcycle. Organised for individual or group trips per hour, or daily with a great guide who'll make sure you'll have a great experience. Look for Ural Tours on Facebook and find out why such a tour is worth booking and experiencing.

Paragliding:

If you are passionate about beautiful views and you love adrenaline, then paragliding is an activity you don't have to miss while in Moldova. It costs only 20euro a flight, it lasts 10-15 minutes and it takes place above a variety of beautiful landscapes such as Orheiul Vechi, Anenii Noi and Dubasari. There are over 30 professionals around the country that can provide such experiences, but the easiest to reach is Vasile Fornea from Parapanta Moldova (see the Facebook page with the same name) or directly at the Paragliding Association in Moldova (see the Facebook page with the same name).

Cycling:

Being widely used abroad as a means of transportation, in Moldova cycling still tries to make its way into mainstream. With more and more enthusiasts and popped up even in the tourism scene, now offering tours in the city, at wineries and even across the country by bicycles. One of the main companies that provide this is **Velopoint** where you can rent a bike and bike equipment per hour. You can find biking routes and customise your trip by contacting the directly on their website www.velopoint.md.

Parachute Jumping:

Skydivers do not have to seek far as in Vadul lui Voda is based the most famous point for that. Every weekend they provide these opportunities, with prices starting from 55 euros according to the Parachutism Association of Moldova. You have options for jumping by yourself or with an instructor, also a variety of specific techniques and equipment including the wing suit. The best experience in skydiving you will get with Skydive Moldova. Feel free to check out their website for more information: www.skydive.md

Hot Air Baloon Rides:

We may not compete with the stunning sights of Cappadocia in Turkey, but we've got our own beauty to be discovered. A ride with the Air balloon is easily organised but it depends how much are you ready to pay for this pleasure. A trip with the balloon per person is 99 euro in a mixed group with the date and time of the flight being set up by the company. If it is a matter of pleasure and not a financial matter then you can choose to pay 349 euro and to decide the date and time of the flight and it requires a group of maximum 4 people. There are 2 companies to which you can address in case you'd like to experience this adventure: Aerobis (www.aerobis.md) and Aerolux (www. aerolux.md)

Rock Climbing:

Even though there are no mountains in Moldova, there are still a couple of places where rock climbing is possible. Butuceni in Orheiul Vechi area is the most common one, with X-style company organising often such events there. If you are looking to book such an experience, check out their events page or contact them directly on their Facebook page.

13. Visiting Moldova in Winter:

Even if in Winter Moldova is less visited, this season has its own charms and perks. Moldovan winters are unpredictable. You can have a lot of warm sunny days with the temperatures above zero, but you can get also low temperatures with or without snow. Although when the snow falls it is magic. You can get temperatures as low as -25 degrees Celsius although it doesn't last for long time, just for a couple of days. Due to such weather conditions, if you plan to visit Moldova in winter please keep in mind the following things:

• Dress up warm: hat or something to have your head covered, gloves, scarf, winter jacket, water resistant, non slippery shoes.

• If driving, you have to be very careful as the roads are icy and slippery and in the city and across the country

• Some areas are more difficult to reach due to snow and ice(hiking areas specifucaly) and some historical monument are closed for visiting in winter, for example Soroca fortress

• Due to unpredictable weather some tours, events and roads can be close so try to be flexible and expect changes in your program.

Now let's speak about what is actually going on in winter in Moldova, what you can see, what you can do and how does It look like. Beginning with the 1st of December, Chisinau gets ready for the winter holidays, it changes colours and atmosphere, it becomes like in fairytales, because every restaurant, bar, shop, tries to decorate it in the most unusual and enjoyable way. So everyone gets ready for the winter holidays period as in Moldova it is quite a long one.

Every year starting the 15th of December and till the 15th of January there is a Christmas Market opened. City center is decorated by the local authorities and each year it is different. The main Christmas tree is installed in the front of the Government building, a little family fair you can see in front of the Opera and Ballet Theatre, and the Christmas Market on the 31st August 1989 street. You will find a variety of activities to occupy your time here. From merry-go-round to booths with traditional Moldova pies and food, hot wine with sugar and pepper called "Izvar" snacks and sweets, traditional goods made from leather and wool. Plenty of balloons and funny toys for kids. On weekends on the main stage situated near the main Christmas tree there are usually live concerts of folk winter songs but also modern music. If you'll look around you will see plenty of special arranged decorations for photo shooting. You can take pictures yourself but there are also professional photographers who for a fee will take great pictures of you and your family or friends. There is also an Ice ring for those who enjoy ice skating.

If speaking the other localities, parts of Moldova, each of them offer their own entertainment. As we've mentioned before, Moldovans are very traditional and they love doing something unusual for the holidays, decorating their houses, preparing their traditional food and inviting guests to enjoy all of these together. Of course in the villages you will not have as many events going on as in the bigger cities, although there you can feel and see the old traditions for the winter holidays. Nowadays only in the villages around Christmas you can see children going from one house to another carolling. Then around New Year with the "Sorcova" "Plugusorul" to bless the houses they visit. These are traditional songs wishing a prosperous new year and god blessing for the owners of the house they visit. They all wear specific traditional clothes and have with them a traditional element like a handmade star. If you'll decide to stay overnight in a village, maybe you'll get to sleep on a "Soba", Moldovan traditional heating system which warms up not just the house and the stove but also you can use it as a bed, on which you can have a good night sleep. In the daytime you can join the children to ride the sledges or if available in that area maybe you can have a ride with a horse sledge.

The winter holiday season ends around 14th of January as on the 13th of January Moldovans celebrate Old New Year. Yes, you've got it right, being in Moldova for winter holidays you get to celebrate Christmas two times and New Year 2 times (25 of December - Christmas; 7th of January – Christmas; 1st of January – New Year; 14th of January – Old New Year). The rest of the January tents to be calm, and then February comes, bringing two holidays celebrating Love: Valentine's Day on the 14th of February and Dragobete on the 24th of February. Most restaurants, bars, clubs and even wineries make various offer, concerts and events to celebrate these holidays, so you won't get bored either.

14. Traditional Holidays in Moldova:

Martisor:

Spring comes with one of the most beautiful holidays on the 1st of March called "Martisor" pronunciation: [mərtsi'ʃor]. It is a holiday that celebrates the rebirth of life after the hard winter. On this day men offer to their beloved women flowers and martisors (the symbol of serenity and happiness).

There are a few legends that explain this ancient beautiful tradition:

One of the old Romanian legends says that once in a fight with the winter witch, that didn't want to give up its place, the beautiful lady Spring cut her finger and few drops of her blood fall on the snow, which melt. Soon on this place grew a snowdrop and in such a way the spring won the winter.

Another legend tells that there was a time when the Sun used to take the shape of a young man and descend on Earth to dance among folk people. Now a dragon found out about this and followed the Sun on Earth, captured him and confined him in a dungeon in his castle. Suddenly the birds stopped singing and the children could not laugh anymore but no one dared to confront the dragon. One day a brave young man set out to find the dungeon and free the Sun. Many people joined in and gave him strength and courage to challenge the mighty dragon.

The journey lasted three seasons: summer, autumn and winter. At the end of the third season the brave young man could finally reach the castle of the dragon where the Sun was imprisoned. The fight lasted several days until the dragon was defeated. Weakened by his wounds the brave young man however managed to set the Sun free to the joy of those who believed in him. Nature was alive again, people got back their smile but the brave young man could not make it through spring. His warm blood was draining from his wounds in the snow. With the snow melting, white flowers, called snowdrops, harbingers of spring, sprouted from the thawing soil. When the last drop of the brave young man's blood fell on the pure white snow he died with pride that his life served a noble purpose.

Since then people braid two tassels: one white and one red. Every March 1 men offer this amulet called Martisor to the women they love. The red color symbolizes love for all that is beautiful and also the blood of the brave young man, while white represents purity, good health and the snowdrop, the first flower of spring.

Literally Martisor means little March: a small trinket pinned on the lapel by which winter is parted and spring is welcomed.

Since 1967, the Martisor musical festival is held from March 1st to 10th in Chisinau, the Republic of Moldova's capital. Members of amateur art groups and professional performers from other countries are invited to take part in the festival.

8th of March – International Women's Day:

Moldova, like most countries, celebrates International Women's day on 8th march and it is also a declared national holiday. Custom holds that men give flowers to women on this day most especially to mothers and grandmothers, as well as to female friends and co-workers. The traditional flowers to offer on this day are the Tulips as they are considered the flowers of spring.

Easter:

Easter is usually celebrated in April or beginning of May, each year it is different but it is a very beautiful holiday because it is in spring and because of the traditions. In Moldova Easter is celebrated 3 days that is why women are very busy with preparation one week before the holiday.

The celebration of Easter begins with the liturgy in church. It begins in the middle of the night at 00:00 in every church in Moldova. If you'd like to assist at the liturgy it is recommended to come a little bit earlier, because there is the chance that you'll stay outside as the churches usually are overcrowded in the holy night.

Every year the Gracious fire is brought from Jerusalem to Moldova in the holy Night. Officials of the country, priests and common people wait for the fire in the central cathedral in Chisinau. The candles are lit from this very fire brought from Jerusalem. Then the candles as the symbol of faith and blessing go to many other churches, monasteries and houses through all the country of Moldova. After the end of the liturgy the priest consecrated all dishes, brought to the church by the believers, according to the tradition people come to the church with a basket full of traditional "Pasca" Easter cake or "cozonac" dyed eggs in red coulor, salt and a bottle of wine.

Coming out of the church when the liturgy ends believers exchange a triple kiss and greet each other with the words "Hristos a Inviat" – "Christ is risen" and the answer to this being "Cu adevarat a Inviat" – "Truly he is risen"

Easter celebration starts when coming back home from church. As mentioned above traditional "Pasca" and Easter cake are baked beforehand on Thursday of the Holy Week. On Saturday of the Holy Week the entire cooking job is done and also the traditional eggs dying. The next three days people will go visit each other, eat drink and have fun. While in Moldova for Easter you have to take care of your stomach because Moldovan traditional food is delicious but it is not easy to digest for those who are not used to.

Easter table is full of traditional dishes but the main dish for Easter it the lamb it is cooked following different recipes, while the main remains to cook it in the oven. Of course there will be rabbit, ham, "sarmale" and many other delicious dishes. Each housewife tries to cook a variety of dishes in order to prove that she is a good cook and the Holy celebration has come and three days no one cooks, everyone eats drinks and have fun.

The museum of Nature and Ethnography traditionally organizes the Easter exhibition, the main competition of artists painting eggs. Famous artisans from Moldova, Ukraine and Romania come here to show their talents. Any visitor can participate in a master-class on painting eggs.

. . .

1ˢᵗ of May – Labour Day:

Labour Day – is an annual holiday to celebrate the achievements of workers and as in the most countries it is a day off. In Moldova people usually go out on this day to celebrate it outdoors with friends and family for a barbeque party.

9ᵗʰ of May – Victory Day:

Victory Day is the day to commemorate the end of World War II. It is the day on which the Nazi Germany defeat is celebrated, also commemorating the victims of this war. It is also the day to honour the World War II veterans who are still alive.

1ˢᵗ of June – Children's Day:

Children's Day is one of the most pleasant and positive holiday because children are celebrated. Lots of activities, presents and free ice cream are available for children all over the country. This is the day when you can see everyone happy, even the grownups as they tend to take part in the activities organised for children.

27ᵗʰ of August – Independence Day:

Independence Day is the national day of Moldova commemorating the adoption of the Declaration of Independence from the Soviet Union on 27 August 1991. Moldovans are happy to be independent that is why concerts are organised in the city centre; people are wearing national clothes and Moldovan national flag.

.   .   .

31ˢᵗ of August – Language Day:

It is the day when the national language is celebrated through songs and poems of well knows poets and young talents.

National Wine Day:

National Wine Day is celebrated in the beginning of October the date changing each year depending on the organizers. This is the largest holiday dedicated to the millennial tradition in winemaking; it calls for discovering the Moldovan Wine Legend with Protected Geographical Indication. In general about 60 wine producers present their product of national pride and the national traditions in winemaking. All the visitors of the event are encouraged to get to know the Wine of Moldova and to enjoy it moderately and responsibly. You can experience the **Wine School** – the best sommeliers guide the participants through the mystery of conscious consumption of Moldovan Wine and organize master classes. Also you can taste the best types of local food prepared during the event, assorted with Moldovan Wine and seasoned with artistic shows with all types of music. Well-known folk music orchestras, dancing clubs from Chisinau and Moldovan regions and local music bands are usually present at the event to entertain the public with their performance. You can also have a look at the **Crafts market** which include exhibitions and workshops of traditional craftsmen, as well as other activities which reveal Moldovan traditions and values.

And then, winter comes full of holidays as mentioned above in the paragraph "Visit Moldova in Winter". December is a crazy month as everyone goes shopping trying to find the best gifts for their close people, friends and relatives. Children often make greeting cards for their parents. People decorate their houses, trees… At this time holidays are not only in the minds but also in the air. In Chisinau, the capital city, there are many Santa Clauses. In Moldova children call Santa Claus "Mos Craciun". These Santas greet children in the shops, theatres, and just on the streets, everywhere. So, children are the most excited! However these all is preparing… The main event still follows!

"Sfintul Nicolae" - "Saint Nicolas" it is celebrated on the 19th of December and it brings candies to all the children who behaved well during the whole year. In the evening before going to bed they have to clean their shoes, the legend says that Saint Nicolas comes and fills the shoes with sweets if you deserve, if not, you will find your shoes empty and there will be a lace, meaning that you were nasty and you won't get any sweets this year. Children are very excited in the morning running to check their shoes hoping that they will get some sweets.

Christmas – Although it is considered as an official day off, not everyone celebrates Christmas on the 25th of December, mainly in Chisinau and other towns, but in the villages they keep the old tradition and they celebrate Christmas on the 7th of January. It is an amazing holiday celebrated with warmth and joy, because it brings families and friends together. If you want to feel the magic of this holiday, you have to spend it in a Moldovan family, this is going to be an experience that you will never forget.

New Year – As mentioned above this holiday is also spent two times in Moldova on the 1st of January and on the 14th of January. Moldovans love winter holidays, they exchange presents with the loved ones eat and drink together, sing traditional songs and dance. There are a lot of interesting activities organised in the city centre, as mentioned in the paragraph "Visit Moldova in Winter".

TRANSNISTRIA AND GAGAUZIA

mysteries and a place of great interest for the tourists, everyone wants to visit Transnistria – a piece of territory that has been autonomous since 1992 and is stuck in a frozen conflict. Most embassies advise not to visit it as it is considered a dangerous country, has the Russian military, and the necessary border control, Transnistria has created quite an image for itself. But let's see if it's really that dangerous.

Historically Transnistria became a state of its own on the 2nd of

September 1990 when it was proclaimed "Dnestrian Moldovan Republic" right after the fall of communism. As Moldova gained its independence in 1991 and was registered as a member of UN on the 2nd of March 1992, it signed a military intervention in the region to get rid of the rebel forces that have been taking over. After a few months of war, on the 21st of July 1992 Moldova signed an agreement of peace with Russia. Till nowadays Russia keeps its military in this region. It is very much connected with Russia: politically, economically and symbolically. Even the Transnistrian flag bears sickle and hammer, leaving no doubts which team the republic is.

Nowadays Transnistria is a place of great interest for the tourists but before going there there are a couple of things you should be aware of. They have their own passport and currency. In order to enter the region you'll be required to register at the border control with a valid passport (you don't need a visa) which is done quite fast and easy there is no need for bribery. Due to the fact that in the last years the flux of tourists increased they even speak a little bit of English at the border now. You will be given a piece of paper on which the duration of your stay will be written, so make sure to stick to that, in case you stay longer than just during the day, make sure to mention that, you will also have to inform the address where you are going to spend the night. Do not lose this paper, as you will need it in order to exit the region.

1. Getting from Chisinau to Transnistria:

Transnistria is only 1h 30min away from Chisinau,if you choose driving with the local mini buses from the central bus station. From the central market, where the central bus station is located they leave each 30 minutes in the direction of Bender and Tiraspol. A ride will cost you 40 lei (2 euros). Of course you can chose to go by taxi which is also possible but will cost you much more expensive, depending on the agency that you will contact, when calling to order a taxi, it is better to ask how much it is going to cost you this trip, as it is a distance and the drivers may ask you to pay a little bit more then the real price. Of course you can rent a car, a private driver or a tour guide. You can also take the train, the one departing to Odessa every Friday, Saturday, Sunday (+Thursday during summer period). It leaves at 6:57 AM from Chisinau.

The first city after passing the border is Bender. Places to visit here are the Military Cemetery and The Memorial of Military Glory which both are situated in the center of the city near the "Praga" stop, which you can request to the minibus driver. A bit further just before approaching the Bender bus station there is the "Bender Fortress" which is situated right on the shore of river Dniestr. It was built in the 14th centuryunder the Moldovan ruler Stefan cel Mare, and later conquered by the Turcs and reconstructed under the Suleyman the Magnificent's order. Since then this fortress was witness to various wars between the Turcs, Russians and even became a retreat location for 4 years for Carl XII, king of Sweeden. Please remember that Transnistria has their own local currency, so if you wish to pay your entrance at the fortress or museum or anything else you'll need their local roubles, which you can find at any exchange point in Chisinau before leaving for the trip to Transnistria. The entrance at the fortress is 50 roubles.

Other things of interest in Bender might be the local market or the flea market near the bus station, the USSR canteen or those target shooting places named as "Tir"(which can also be found at the fortress).

Even if Bender and Tiraspol are separated by the river, they are united by the famous Dniestr bridge and they have the trolleybus 19 or 19a that connects both these cities. A ride costs 3 roubles.

2. Places to visit in Tiraspol:

Tiraspol is the second largest city of Moldova. Only Chisinau has more cultural monuments and entertainment venues than Tiraspol. The city was named after the Dniester River that sounds like «Tyras» in Greek. Tiraspol gained its name right after the foundation, at the end of the 18th century, when the so-called "Greek Project" of Catherine II was incredibly popular.

The territory of the city came to the Russian Empire only in 1791, after the Russian-Turkish War. To strengthen the new border, it was decided to form a new city in 1792. Upon the order of A. V. Suvorov, the fortress was built. Tiraspol gained the status of the city in 1795. It flourished only in the second half of the 19th century. The railway made the developing craft center an important economic object. The items manufactured here were exported to the largest trading platforms of the county. The local craftsmen's items were very popular at different fairs. Several big fairs took place exactly in Tiraspol. The active development of the city was ceased by the First World War. It was also seriously damaged during the Great Patriotic War. It took the locals over 10 years to restore their native city. Today, it is not only a flourishing economic and industrial center, but also an attractive tourist place.

At the entrance you will be greeted by the famous Sheriff Stadium which next to it has a supermarket and a gas station under the same name.

Tourists from distant cities and countries are attracted by the inimitable atmosphere of the city and its wonderful nature. The Dniester Valley has long been an attractive place for fans of ecotourism. There is just no better place for hiking and recreation. Many attractive natural sites are located in the immediate surroundings of Tiraspol. In the lively city streets, there are very interesting cultural sites and entertainment venues. The city will impress not only those who love sightseeing tours and nature places, but also fans of Soviet films. Many popular Soviet films were shot exactly in Tiraspol. It should be noted that the cult streets and avenues of the city have not almost changed since that time.

In Tiraspol, you can take an interesting sightseeing tour. In the beautiful historic building with a tiled roof, there is the Tiraspol Unified Museum. In the first half of the city, several small museums were founded in the city. Then, it was decided to unify them. The Unified Museum was opened in 1958. Now, several themed exhibitions are organized here. Some of them are dedicated to important historical events, other cultural traditions, and lifestyle of citizens. In total, the museum collection contains of over 100 000 exhibits.

Chitcani Monastery is located on a small hilltop. It was founded in the second half of the 19th century. The monastery is quite a big architectural complex. On its territory, there are four old temples and several outbuildings. One of the historic buildings serves as a church museum and an old library with rare books. The monastery is distinguished by beautiful adjacent area. There are several excellent viewing platforms.

A very important post war monument that you have to see while in Tiraspol is the Council House which was built in 1953. Now the building with columns belonged to the city council and is closed for visitors, so the city guests can always admire only its exterior. There is a beautiful square in front of the building. In a warm period, it is decorated with lush flower beds.

Among the important religious monuments, the Cathedral of the Transfiguration of the Saviour is worth being mentioned. It started to be built in 1815 and was finished in 5 years. Originally, it was distinguished not only by its magnificent exterior, but also with its luxurious interior design. One of the main decorations of the monastery is the big carved iconostasis. Its inner design has a lot of unique features. Many people intend to visit the monastery on a sunny day to admire the unusual gleam in the bell tower. In this gleam, you can see the trellis of yellow rays. This is a characteristic feature of only one church in the world, and it is located in Italy. You should definitely visit the Tiraspol Fortress that was built in the late 18th century. It was a starting point in the city foundation. Nowadays, only some fragments of the magnificent fortress have survived to this day. The entire territory of the fortress is open for visitors.

If you would like to try some local specialities you can stop by the local market and taste from the great variety of pickled vegetables – cabbage, tomatoes, cucumber but also you should try pickled apples and watermelon, yes it sounds weird but it tastes great. While here you should probably visit Kvint Distillery one of the most famous brandy factory but the booking should be done at least 5 days in advance.

But Transnistria does not end here, besides Bender and Tiraspol there are other cities too.

In the village Tirnauca you can visit the "Bottle Museum" which is a private museum founded in 1988 and hosts around 20.000 bottles from over 170 countries. Staying overnight is also possible in their hotel giving you the opportunity to get to know the village and taste their alcohol. Nearby Tiraspol, in Chitcani you can visit the beautiful monastery Noul Neamt which is a monk monastery and it provides overnight stays.

If you are willing to drive more up north the region then you can visit Grigoriopol, Dubasari, Ribnita which is considered the North Transnistrean capital. In Dubasari you can visit "Buket Moldavii" factory, which produces vermouth, sparkling wines, liqueurs, bitters, brandy and balsams – one of them being the balsam "Cosmic" the famous balsam that was taken in space by the Russian astronauts in Soviet Union.

Beautiful spots of Transnistria can also be observed from the left shore of Molovata, Saharna, Japca Monsatery which a situated on Moldovan territory. During the warm seasons boat rides can be booked along the Dniestr river, which will give you the opportunity to see both shores.

Whatever you decide to visit during your trip, it's going to be an experience that you will never forget, as it is a dip into the Soviet past.

3. Visit Gagauzia:

Gagauzia is an autonomous region of Moldova although there is no border to cross as in Transnistria and you don't have to exchange money, they use "Lei" as in the rest of the country. Ethnically Gagauzians are Turkic, with their ancestors coming all the way from Altai region. Later on they migrated from Bulgaria together with ethnic Bulgarian and Settled in Bessarabia (Moldova) between 1812 and 1846. Nowadays the region is comprised of one city, two towns, twenty villages and three communities. Despite their turikc roots, the most interesting fact is that they are affiliated with the Eastern Orthodox Church.

They have their own language which is taught in 55 schools, although Gagauz is still not used as the language of instruction in educational institutions. The official languages in Gagauzia are Russian and Romanian and the majority of population choose to speak Russian language.

If you plan to visit Gagauzia during your stay in Moldova, here are some suggestions on what to see and experience.

In Comrat you can visit the National History and Etnographic Museum the entrance will cost you 10 lei. It has a collection of historical, cultural and even botanical exhibits. Nearby you will find monuments of the fallen soldiers in Afganistan and the tankists, Comrat Art Gallery which showcases local Gagauzian art, the Cathedral, Turkish library Mustafa Kemal Ataturk and of course Victory square where you will see the statue of Lenin right in front of their administrative building. Also in the city you can find the Comrat Winery which is their main wine producer.

Heading more South to Besalma village for th Etnographic Museum where you can discover all the history of the Gagauz nation in a wonderful collection. Unfortunatelly the local guide makes the tour only in Russian, so when visiting the museum it would be great to have a translator with you. If booked upfront, they can organise a little concert also with their national music, traditional costumes and dances.

If you are interested or maybe passionate about Soviet style, then in the post office across the street from the museum you will find interesting postcards that will be by your liking. An office where you can send letters, pay your bills, but also buy things from the counter, just like in soviet times, you can still felt there. The villagers are very friendly and will be very happy to try to speak to you even with the language barrier. A few meters through the village and you can see the Besalma windmill, one of the last ones in Moldova.

The biggest and most condensed village in Europe is Congaz, here you can discover Gagauzian traditional specialities – Gagauz Sofrasi. This is a traditional gagauz style hose which offers local food, lodging but also different kind of experiences, like attending a traditional wedding, milking the sheep, wine tasting and even trying out therapeutic sheep wool beds. Keep in mind that they cater for groups of minimum 4 people and require a 24 hours upfront booking.

4. KaraGani Winery:

And last but not least, deep in the south of Moldova about 3 hours drive from Chisinau is the KaraGani Winery. It is only 200 km from Chisinau, near the Ukranian border in the city of Vulcanesti. It is a name rather new on the Moldovan wine market but not one to be missed, that's for sure.

The tradition of winemaking in the Cereven family comes all the way from their gagauzian ancestors. As the craft for wine was passed down over 4 generations, the wife Lora and husband Gheorghe took their passion a few steps further, developing it into a bussines. They started producing their wine for the public only 2 years ago; they have already gained various recognitions and awards at local and international contests.

Eachyesr they produce only 10.000 bottles for public consumption which can be purchased in a few shops across the capital, Comrat and also directly from them at the winery. The production process can be seen during an excursion as they take you through the whole process and a visit in autumn guarantees you to watch and even participate in their production.

Besides winemaking, they also offer a peek into Gagauzian traditional life in their own, self made museum which consists of objects gathered throughout the years by their families. You will see there from pictures of their relatives to old irons, lamps, Gagauzian furniture, handmade carpets and a trunk full of grandmother's wedding dowry will leave you impressed and gasping for more stories.

Wine tasting at KaraGani is a must and the basic tasting package comes with 3 wines, including one white, one red and one rose. While you are enjoying the wines, Lora of Gheorghe will tell you various stories about each wine and their history.

The price for the excursion which includes wine tasting (3 types of wine) will cost you 150 lei (7 euros) and it lasts for one hour. For those wishing to immerse themselves deeper into the Gagauzian culture, Lora offers the option of tasting their national cuisine with delicacies like homemade cheese, gozleme and their famous lamb dishes –

kaurma, shurpa etc. Such delicacy to enjoy lasts 3 hours and will cost you 25 euros including the excursion and the wine tasting of 4 wine types. Master classes are also available for those that wish to to learn both their cooking and wine making crafts. Such options need to be discussed and booked upfront at least one day before your arrival.

Visiting such a small winery will be something memorable as you get to experience the authentic Moldova – a local family producing wine in their own yard. And how does their wine have a Gagauzian accent (as they state in their company slogan) it something that you will have to discover by yourself.